THE
LITTLE
WORLD
OF
LAOS

BOOKS BY ODEN MEEKER

ODEN MEEKER

THE
LITTLE
WORLD
OF
LAOS

WITH A PICTURE ESSAY BY
HOMER PAGE

CHARLES SCRIBNER'S SONS   NEW YORK

About one-third of this book has been expanded from an article entitled "Don't Forget Madame's Elephant" in *The Saturday Evening Post*, copyright 1956 by The Curtis Publishing Company.

THIS BOOK PUBLISHED SIMULTANEOUSLY IN THE UNITED STATES OF AMERICA AND IN CANADA— COPYRIGHT UNDER THE BERNE CONVENTION

A–1.59 [V]

PRINTED IN THE UNITED STATES OF AMERICA

Library of Congress Catalog Card Number 59-6175

ACKNOWLEDGEMENTS

All of the photographs were taken by Homer Page with the exception of the following which are reproduced courtesy of the UNITED STATES INFORMATION SERVICE:

1. A plane drops food to refugees.
2. The Crown Prince leaves one of the grottoes.
3. The Royal Ballet performs the Ramayana.

The photographs of "the boy bonzes in the pagodas" and "the antique water buffaloes" were taken by the author.

TO MY MOTHER

KATHARINE ODEN HUGHART MEEKER

CONTENTS

7

8　CONTENTS

INTRODUCTION

It was a bright November day with a nip in the air, warm in the sun, cold in the shadows. The sky was a shining, clear, pale blue with touches of white like the United Nations flag flying in its own territory a couple of blocks north. Warren Pinegar and I were walking up First Avenue on our way to lunch. A slight, blond, nervous, compassionate, and efficient man who is now the United Nations Deputy High Commissioner of Refugees, he was then director of all CARE's overseas operations. His desk was piled with stacks of paper from various parts of the world, but that day he was mainly concerned with Laos.

We were supposed to be talking about possible CARE programs in Africa. I had spent most of the past four years immersed in African studies, and was supposed to say something intelligent. But Warren suddenly asked me, "How would you like to go to Laos?" A few hours later I found myself being shot —like a pea from a pea shooter—through the CARE machinery.

I knew that CARE was a private relief agency set up by a couple of dozen American social service organizations at the end of the Second World War to send parcels of food and tools to people in Europe. Gradually, as some of the European countries got back on their feet, and CARE's programs reached out to the Latin Americas, the Middle East, and Asia, it had been obliged to change its unwieldy official title from Co-operative

9

for American Remittances to Europe, Inc., to Co-operative for American Relief to Everywhere, Inc.

At the same time, I was trying to fill out personnel forms, insurance forms, fidelity bond forms, and just plain forms. I had a couple of physical check-ups, and my teeth filled. I tried quickly to pick up a few things with which to go halfway around the world for a year or two. CARE got me a new passport illustrated with what I believe to be a picture of Dorian Gray. CARE flew me to Washington for Vietnamese and Lao visas, bought me a typewriter with a polyglot keyboard and a supply of traveler's checks, produced an international driver's licence in English, French, Spanish, Russian, and Chinese, and had me given shots for tetanus, typhoid, typhus, cholera, and yellow fever. Plague, they said, I could get in the Far East.

Why did I want to go to Laos for CARE—instead of, say, joining the Red Cross, or writing a book about Puerto Rican Harlem? Mostly, I think, because I had spent the greater part of the past ten years in the hot, old-but-new countries of the Latin Americas and of Africa south of the Sahara, with an interlude in northern and western Europe, and had become increasingly concerned with the twin tides of race and nationalism. This was a chance to see a part of the changing Asian world, try to understand if I could the similarities and the differences and the common denominator between that world and the world of color in the Americas, in Africa, and at home in the United States.

It was important that I was going for CARE. For several years now I had been growing increasingly uneasy, feeling more and more like the Russian novelists' "superfluous man." Occasionally I tried to write something useful, but the more misery and trouble I saw around the world, the more my conscience bothered me. Doing a small, daily job for CARE, I thought, would at least be useful.

THE
 LITTLE
 WORLD
 OF
 LAOS

1 THE WAY EAST

INDOCHINA is so far away from New York that it costs just about as much to fly there by circling the earth one way as it does the other. At the crossroads between Indian and Chinese cultures, the Kingdom of Laos is a constitutional monarchy within the French Union, one of the three independent states which together used to make up French Indochina—four now, including the Vietminh's Communist state in North Vietnam. In late 1954, when I left New York, a fair number of Americans had heard of Vietnam; that spring America, with most of the rest of the world, had followed daily the long and desperate French defense of its northern Vietnamese stronghold at Dienbienphu until it finally fell on the seventh of May under the pounding of Vietminh and Chinese artillery from the surrounding heights. But few non-Laotians had yet heard of Laos, a few miles from Dienbienphu, and twice during the

13

two preceding years invaded by the Vietminh. Most people's reaction to the name of Laos was that of my mother: when I announced dramatically that I was going to Laos, she said, "That's very nice, dear. Where is it?"

Well, Laos is an elongated land of less than a hundred thousand square miles bounded by Thailand on the west and touched by Burma on the northwest, by China to the north, by Vietnam to the east and southeast, and by Cambodia on the southwest. The Mekong River, which marks most of the twelve-hundred-mile western frontier with Thailand, is placid but considerable, a little longer than the Mississippi. Up beyond the green gorges of the southwest Chinese province of Yunnan, its headwaters are fed by the melting snows of Tibet. And until recently the Lao kingdom of the river's middle reaches was nearly as isolated as the Roof of the World, and not half so well publicized. The *a* in Laos is soft as in "ah." The adjective is Laotian or Lao. The people are Laotians or Lao. Actually the inhabitants call everything simply Lao, but for some mysterious reason the French elected to make the word plural.

Anywhere from a million to four million people live in Laos, depending on who is making the estimate. But it is agreed that they are dreamy, gentle, bucolic, nonaggressive people, Buddhists of the Little Vehicle who live in bamboo-and-thatch houses on stilts, wading tranquilly in their marshy paddies, fishing in the lazy rivers, and worshiping in the curly-roofed pagodas. They are content. They live in a subsistence economy, and generally there is enough rice to go around. The Lao gentleness traditionally has enchanted the foreign visitor, particularly one not trying to go anywhere or do anything in a hurry. Especially the French, beginning with Captain Cupet, a member of the Pavie expedition of the 1880s that brought Laos within the French orbit. The captain was fascinated by these people *"si douces, si paisables et si confiantes, que la gaité n'abondonne jamais, même dans les pires malheurs."*

Laos, I read, had no railroads. During the rainy season from around April through September it was impossible to travel overland from the capital province to any of the eleven others. This meant that if there should happen to be crop failure in one area, it was next to impossible to bring in surplus food from another.

This had happened twice in a row in parts of Laos following the Vietminh invasions. There were reports that in some places people were eating roots and the bark of trees. Bands of ragged refugees fleeing the Communist-held areas were streaming over the mountains to sanctuary. They needed help—food first of all—and this was what had brought CARE to Laos.

The reigning monarch of Laos, King Sisavang Vong, though only in his early seventies, had been longer on the throne than anyone else in the business. His dynasty had ruled half a millennium and more, and was younger only than that of Japan. It was the relatively mild Japanese occupation which had shaken this peaceable land out of its tranquil acceptance of the world, or as much of it as filtered through, and led to the postwar demand for Laotian independence. There was a brief scuffle with the French, which was patched up satisfactorily for most Lao, but the last-ditchers within the independence movement, the Lao Issara, had refused to come to terms, had finally picked up support from the Vietminh, and had served as a screen for the Communist thrusts into Laos in 1952 and 1953. These dissidents, who called themselves the Pathet Lao, ended up in control of most of the two northern Lao provinces of Phongsaly and Samneua, bordering on China and North Vietnam. At the Geneva Conference in the late summer of 1954, the Vietminh were awarded that half of Vietnam north of the 17th parallel. Under the International Commission for Supervision and Control in Laos—composed of Indians, Canadians, and Poles—Communist forces were supposed to regroup themselves in specified areas, and then disperse. Those in the north of Laos had set up a rustic Communist state, theoretically acknowledging the crown but refusing its administration. There were sporadic clashes between the Royal and the Pathet Lao forces, and the doomsayers predicted that the Kingdom of Laos would fall to the Communists, with Thailand, Burma, Cambodia, Malaya, and Singapore toppling after it like dominoes. Thoughtful but less alarmist observers feared that Laos was in the most precarious position of all the non-Communist states of Asia. Though CARE is nonpolitical, all this didn't make it any easier to meet a national emergency.

The quickest way to Saigon from New York was on one of Air France's express services out of Paris, and as we droned through the night on a Super Constellation with the little blue flying seahorse painted on its nose, I wondered how I had ever made the connection. On a Tuesday, CARE had asked me how long it would take to get ready to leave for Indochina, and when I replied, oh, perhaps three weeks or so, suggested gently that I might take off the following Saturday. I did. Madeleine Brennan, the literary agent, rallied to the cause and subcontracted shopping assignments; the novelist Hilde Abel went steaming out to buy two-years-in-the-tropics' worth of kaolin, paregoric, merthiolate, Band-Aids, insect repellent, fungicide, prickly heat powder, sock stretchers, and miracle fabric drip-drying shirts. There were family things like birth-days and Thanksgiving, and jet-propelled Christmas shop-ping. There were no white suits to be had in New York, but an outfitter promised to produce some by air parcel. I took them, but they made me look like one of Al Capp's zoot-suiters. I tried to assemble a basic library of reference books to ship to Indochina. I was shopping for sunglasses, and red-paper Santa Clauses at Dennison's at the same time.

Friday night Maddy Brennan gave a party. The next day she and her roommate Bertie Moore and Bertie's small black poodle Bébert drove me to the airport. Then, at the last mo-ment, we were caught in a traffic jam on the way to Idlewild. We were stopped dead for nearly an hour. Bébert made friends with another poodle in a nearby motionless car. Maddy calmly produced a hamper with an excellent picnic lunch, and offered us a choice between a milk punch and a dry martini.

2 SAIGON

WELLS CAMPBELL KLEIN, then CARE's chief of mission in Vietnam, was waiting for me at the airport in Saigon. He was a tallish, friendly, intense, efficient and highly intelligent, sensitive fellow, with his hair brushed back in a long crew cut, and with disconcertingly steady gray eyes. At twenty-eight, he was a veteran CARE man who had already fed two and a half million people regularly during a famine in Yugoslavia, and as a bachelor was much pursued by an international array of young women, one of whom told me to be sure not to miss that bit about the eyes.

Saigon was steaming hot, as hot and wet as West Africa or the mouth of the Amazon. We drove into town through a suicidal swarm of buses, buglike French cars, and pedicabs, and pulled in at the CARE place, a villa with a tile roof set in a small garden surrounded by a low wall, with a two-room office building at one side. There were five people in the office: Wells' deputy was Jacques Lauriac, a lean young man with a close-cropped shock of black hair and a mobile, saturnine face, always cheerfully expecting the worst to happen. He was born in France, trained as an engineer with Remington Rand, served with the US Army occupation forces in Germany, and had taken out American citizenship. His dream was to go to Brazil, but he found himself in Indochina. Then there was Mr. Ngha, a very slight, older Vietnamese artist who in latter years had been obliged to take up accounting, at which he was very good; and two sensational secretarial sisters, Cantonese from a mercantile family out of Hong Kong, both young, humorous, and somehow cool and crisp in the sweltering heat. During the Japanese occupation they had been refugees in Dalat in central Vietnam, where they went to an excellent convent school called Les Oiseaux. Helen Lau, the elder, was taller, composed, ivory-skinned, and she wore the high-collared, slit-skirt Chinese dress called a *chungsam;* Jane Lau was smaller, browner, merry as a grig, and she wore European skirt and blouse. Both were willing to work on all known holidays, and they operated a gas pump outside the front door of their house on the way to Cholon.

In the garden the Vietnamese government kept an armed guard—sometimes the man who arrived for night duty looked like an admiral, with shoulder boards and white shorts, and he slept in a little tent of mosquito net he rigged up on the garden bench, his gun beside him. There were bars on the windows of the CARE house as there were everywhere in town. The twin cities of Saigon-Cholon both had the jimjams, as did most of Vietnam north and south. In Ho Chi Minh's Democratic Republic of Vietnam to the north of the 17th parallel, everyone was declared to be universally delighted at being liberated, though the port of Haiphong, near Ho's capital at Hanoi, which the Geneva Agreement stipulated must be left open as an escape hatch for three hundred days, was crowded with refugees strong enough and brave enough and lucky enough to make the break for the south. In the end, there were about eight hundred thousand of them—most of them Catholics—who came jammed aboard the French and American ships running a refugee shuttle service down to Saigon. They trooped ashore with their babies and their umbrellas and their coolie hats and the few pitiful possessions they were able to bring with them. They lived in board-and-bamboo tropical shantytowns strung out along the highways, too often subsisting on the dole, with no land to cultivate. Usually there was a simple church surmounted with a bamboo cross—there are some two million Christians among twenty-two millions in all Vietnam, a remarkable proportion in either Asia or Africa.

In Saigon the refugees were crowded into every conceivable corner. Hundreds of families were dossed down in the baroque opera house across the square from the Hotel Continental, squeezed in side by side with their bamboo mats and their cooking pots and their rags of laundry in the shadows of the balcony, the wings, the stage itself, and the orchestra, looking like a vast Dickensian debtors' prison. They were curled up on the streets and in the doorways. Their future and that of everyone else in town was veiled in the feverish uncertainty of the times.

Lord knows what stereotype the outside world had formed of Indochina in general and Saigon in particular: Dienbienphu, with its gallant, terrible—and perhaps unnecessary—fall; Fu Manchu, opium dens, and silken sirens; international intrigue, informers, merchants of death, black marketeers, and double and triple agents of uncertain nationality.

The truth was simpler and really worse: a nation torn by civil war and the struggle for independence, unnaturally cut in two; where the Communists had seized leadership of the early fight for independence from the French; and with nearly three million refugees (the eight hundred thousand from the north and some two million in the south itself who had been driven from their homes as effectively as if they had been a part of the dramatic exodus from the north).

The backdrop was much as painted: the government-licensed factory for processing crude opium was being closed down, it is true, but friends who were economic advisers to the government had recently made a tour of the plant, and been given as souvenirs thin circular brass containers in which the opium was packed. The notorious Madame Jo from Hanoi had arrived and set up shop, and in general the illegal traffic in narcotics seemed to be as great a headache to the colonial authorities as the legal one, but without the revenue. The theoretical head of the country was the Emperor Bao Dai, then called Chief of State, but he dallied interminably on the French Riviera, never returning to Vietnam, apparently prevented by friend and foe and his own nature. Bao Dai had let the gambling, prostitution, and police concessions in Saigon as a package monopoly to a gangster-military group known as the Binh Xuyen, for an alleged twenty-five thousand dollars a day. The Binh Xuyen held the police headquarters on the main street in the center of town, and it was to them one went to have a passport stamped with permission to remain in Vietnam or leave the country. When we visited our warehouse in Cholon, in Binh Xuyen territory, we passed a sort of frontier guarded by a Binh Xuyen soldier wearing a green beret and holding a tommy gun, in front of a sentry box striped with the Binh Xuyen colors.

In addition to the Binh Xuyen (pronounced approximately "Beenzwen"), who were the most troublesome of all in that they controlled the territory around the capital, there were the other feudal religio-military cults which sprang up in the turbulent years following the Japanese occupation. They fought sometimes with the Communists and sometimes against them (the Binh Xuyen spent their first postwar year with the Vietminh), often among themselves, and usually against the French government. From time to time their leaders would ostentatiously rally to the government, promising the loyalty of their troops, accept high rank in the French Army, then go back and start all over again. The commanders of these sects proclaimed themselves nationalist patriots, and usually the prophets of a new religion, but used their power to carve out their own baronial fiefs. There they levied taxes, conscripted soldiers, collected tolls, sold protection, and maintained their own governments complete with layers of bureaucrats, and stoutly refused to let the government of the land into their territories.

The most imposing of the sects was the Cao Dai, whose Pope presided over a syncretism of Buddhism, Taoism, Confucianism, Christianity, animism and spiritualism revealed to the world about 1926. He commanded a standing army of at least fifteen thousand (half the size of the national armies of either of the neighboring states of Laos or Cambodia), and ministered to a flock of a million and a half. His Vatican was at Tay Ninh, sixty-odd miles northeast of Saigon, where Victor Hugo, Sun Yat Sen, Mark Twain, and Napoleon Bonaparte are among the saints in a temple with writhing dragon pillars that is probably the world's finest flowering of Chinese amusement-park décor. The southwest near the Cambodian frontier was the stronghold of the Hoa Hao (roughly, "Wa

How"), a belligerent neo-Buddhist-Brahman sect of nearly a million, which kept twelve thousand men under arms including the young guerilla leader called Ba Cut, who let his hair grow to his shoulders and chopped off a joint of one finger as a gesture of defiance to the foreign rulers of Vietnam. Ba Cut rallied to the French authorities at least four times, reverted to guerilla warfare against them, and ended up on the guillotine of the independent Republic of Vietnam. The officers and men of these feudal levies wore kepis, berets, and French-cut uniforms. They were the latest such religious military groups in the world. They were the contemporary descendents of the Yellow Turbans, the White Lotuses, the Red Eyebrows, and a long line of Southeast Asian secret political-religious societies, and they kept the country in an uproar.

There was sporadic mortar fire at night from the Binh Xuyen across the river from Saigon, and periodically someone would blow up one of the electric substations and plunge a part of the town into darkness. Army tents had sprouted like mushrooms in the grounds around the palace; on a knoll in a gazebo in the neighboring park sat a young soldier holding a submachine gun. A few people were shot in the streets. One of the first things I heard after arriving was an American clubwoman's saying, "It must have been just about this time last year that poor Mr. Parkinson was shot to death in a pedicab." It was true.

The foreign correspondents in town to cover the wars and the extraordinary Operation Exodus by which the refugees were brought from North to South Vietnam were more than professionally skeptical about South Vietnam's chances of survival. Sometimes I joined them sitting on the sidewalk café of the Hotel Continental watching the early evening pass-

ing parade: there were the steady stream of Vietnamese busi-
nessmen in sharp suits; vendors and peasants trotting along,
flat bamboos springing rhythmically on their shoulders, hung
fore and aft with shallow baskets filled with vegetables, plastic novelties, anything and everything. The slender Vietnamese salesgirls and stenos whizzed by on bikes and motor
bikes, their glazed cream-colored palm-leaf hats tied under
their chins with broad black or bright-colored velvet ribbons,
their sheer, bell-bottomed pantaloons and the fronts and
backs of the ankle-length dresses, slit to the waist, all blowing
in the breeze.

There were Americans in cord suits in the crowd, an occasional Chinese amah with her charges on the way to the small
park nearby, white tunic and shiny black floppy pants, strong
flat face, and balding, squarish high forehead, with glossy
pigtails. Some of the male French colonials wore their sausage-
skin short shorts with cuffs, duck-tail Saint-Germain-des-Près
haircuts, and shirts open nearly to the belt, corsair-fashion.
There were a number of fashionably cropped female heads
in the familiar French metallic red. There were a few clipped
French poodles with wide studded collars in canary or scarlet
or jet black.

There were lots of Foreign Legionnaires in town, mostly
young Germans, wearing white cotton sidewalls around their
kepis, and the African troops called Tirailleurs Sénégalais.
Both groups had suffered terrible losses at Dienbienphu. Patrols of Vietnamese, sometimes with French officers, went
briskly past. They aimed to keep the peace, at least in the
center of town. After all, at least one French *colon* had been
shot sipping his *apéritif* here at a Continental sidewalk table,
and an automobile parked beside the hotel in front of the

opera house had been blown up at high noon. It was a time of troubles.

The Sikhs with their flowered turbans and trim beard nets, the smart Indian Navy officers in tropical whites, the Canadians in dark olive-drab battle dress with their sleeves neatly rolled up, and the Poles whose square-crowned dress caps gave them a rather old-fashioned, Mythlvanian look— all were staying at the Continental and one of the other hotels in town as members of the International Control Commission. It was a difficult, exasperating, and thankless job, as usual, with each side accusing the hapless policemen of favoring the other. And the policemen were not only unarmed, they had no authority. If one side were illegally to increase the size of its armed forces and military installations, as happened in North Vietnam, there was no other recourse than to write a protest to Geneva. In practice, the Commission members worked together harmoniously enough—a neutral Indian chairman, with an Eastern Pole and a Western Canadian—but their hands were tied, and there was seldom any way for villagers in the north who wanted to flee to get through to them. Some villages were cruelly punished for daring to try to do so.

It was fashionable among foreigners in Indochina to be critical of the Commission and all its works. But then, it was a time when all groups were bitterly critical of all others, and I am convinced that things would have been even worse had the international patrolmen not been there. To anyone who was at all sensitive to feeling in the world of color, the air of Saigon was bad, bad and jittery. There was a palpable hostility among the Vietnamese toward the French, and this extended, at one remove, to Americans and other palefaced

Westerners. The diehards among the French were furious with the Americans, whom they saw as usurpers pushing them out of Indochina, and undermining them in Algeria. Many Americans were so jaundiced with the French record in Indochina that they sounded as though they despised all things French. On the sidelines of these major antagonisms, the Vietnamese were divided between themselves, and all Vietnamese seemed to join in fearful and violent prejudice against the Chinese population of perhaps a million, who had effectively monopolized the business of the country. The half-million tribesmen who lived in the mountains of central Vietnam and were known by the condescending group title of *Moi,* or "Savages," complained that the Vietnamese discriminated against them. Feeling was perhaps worst in the cities; in a decade of travel through many countries in troubled times, I can't remember feeling myself, as an outsider, the object of an emotional undercurrent of such intense animosity —not in the African slums of Johannesburg during the gang wars, or in Nairobi at the height of the Mau Mau.

CARE'S part in all this was simply to get through as much help as possible to the unending stream of people whose lives had been disrupted. CARE in New York had begun by shipping in a couple of planeloads of antibiotics donated by American manufacturers—the first relief supplies to reach Vietnam after the cease-fire was signed. Condensed milk and then rice and other food began to arrive. There were books for the schools, "welcome kits" of small necessities for refugees, midwifery kits and layettes, carpenter's tools and resettler's agricultural tool kits. Sometimes it was difficult to move supplies when guerilla fighting erupted in an area Wells Klein and his staff were trying to reach, or gangsters or patriots or both began to blow up things between the warehouse and the intended beneficiaries.

My first CARE distribution—the first time I actually watched somebody handing something to somebody else on behalf of CARE's donors—came a couple of days after I reached Saigon, when Wells asked me to come along to the opera house where some University of Hanoi students, refugees themselves, were to help with the distribution of food to others worse off than they. With them, on the steps of the opera house, was a miragelike character, a smiling, square-jawed, clean-cut American boy wearing a Princeton beer jacket: this turned out to be George Lambrakis, from US Information Service, come to lend a hand. And there turned out to be a great deal more to relief work than just handing somebody something. To try to get the right things to the right people at the right time involved all sorts of logistics and procurement problems and careful reporting that explained the battery of machines in New York and CARE's insistence on accountability down to the last bean. Beyond that there was the problem of keeping a large crowd of people in order, often in times of great stress, when nerves were close to the surface. There was the problem of making sure that stocks were decently stored, that those in greatest need were the ones who appeared, and that the distributors didn't try to give everything to their cousins and uncles (after all, it is only natural to try to take care of one's own)—a thousand and one things. I had a lot to learn.

Twenty-eight of the Hanoi University students spent most of the Christmas holidays with Wells and Jacques and me filling in donors' names and addresses on 140,000 labels to be pasted on CARE packages of food going to Vietnam and to

Laos. The labels were pictorial, with an American couple at the left-hand side, a ship steaming across it, and either a Vietnamese or Lao couple with their children on the right. Later we had to change it: few of the landlocked Lao had ever seen a steamship, but they all recognized an airplane.

I was first surprised, and then very much moved, by the remarkable range of people who had contributed their dollars to send the food: they came from all over the United States and Canada, from Fairbanks, Alaska, and from Honolulu, from Germany, from Salon-sur-Saône in France, and from Helsinki.

3 THE PLACE OF SANDALWOOD

SAIGON was running a high fever. There were days when it seemed that the whole place would slide off the brink into chaos. And things would get worse. But over the coming year I was to look forward to occasional working visits for a change of pace if not for a rest. There was no mortar fire at night in Vientiane, the capital of Laos, and the opposition there did not keep you awake by blowing up the neighborhood electric station as they did in Saigon, but living in Laos had its own problems.

I was curious to learn more about Vietnam, for this is the Chinese side of Indochina, just as Laos and Cambodia are the Indian. But there was no time now. Each day the clock had begun to tick a little faster, for CARE's food packages destined for Laos were already at sea, and due shortly to be unloaded at Bangkok and shipped up overland to Vientiane.

Early one morning Wells Klein shepherded me aboard the

American government's weekly courier plane that flew from Saigon to Vientiane, the end of the line. It was an honest working DC-3, on charter from CAT (Civil Air Transport), General Chennault's Nationalist Chinese flag line from Formosa, which had begun as the Flying Tigers in China, branched out into Far Eastern commercial flights, served as certainly part of the inspiration for the comic strip "Terry and the Pirates," and which was now rapidly transforming itself into a highly respectable, international airline, but would still take on any odd job in Asia. This was one of them.

Piloted by one of the veterans of the Dienbienphu run, the CAT courier took off while there was still mist over the fields and paddies. We were on the milk run: forty-five minutes west by northwest over the rich, flat ricelands to Phnom-Penh, the capital of Cambodia, and then on another hour and a half to Bangkok on the Gulf of Siam, and a couple of hours north up through Thailand to the Lao capital of Vientiane on the Mekong. The coolness of the early morning had vanished, and it was already blazing hot by the time we reached Phnom-Penh, standing in the shadow of a wing of the plane, in a field surrounded by other fields while sacks of mail were exchanged, and cargo loaded and unloaded for the American Embassy. Somewhere up the line were the incredible ruins of Angkor Vat. In Bangkok it was a little cooler, and the paved runways and the planes taking off for Hong Kong and Calcutta gave me the feeling we were still in touch with the outside world. Then on up through the eastern Thai province to Laos.

There was still a dash of "Terry and the Pirates" left in CAT. We sat in bucket seats: a few wilted Americans in cord and seersucker—secretaries, economic mission people, the State Department courier, a correspondent from CBS—a couple of lean French colonial civil servants who had obviously spent many years in the tropics, Chinese and Vietnamese domestics with many gold teeth, on their way to join families in Vientiane, and a handful of Lao officials and their wives, short, well knit, smiling gently, and somehow a little detached. Also, a Vietnamese girl who looked as though she were on parole from a dance hall; no one could say exactly how she got on the plane, but they were all interested.

Facing the passengers who were flying sideways was the cargo, cases of condensed milk, a woman's green bicycle, two bright red electric generators, a chemical toilet, a Siamese cat in a wicker cage, all lashed together in a criss-cross of rope secured to rings in the deck and bulkheads. There were canvas sacks, string bags, tin footlockers, and a whale-backed trunk. Below, we could now see mountains, long jagged ridges, half hidden in mist, bluish-white washed with brown and green. We passed the 17th parallel, a little to the west of the uneasy line between the southern Vietnamese and the Communist Vietminh.

Now there was again the jigsaw of rice paddies, winter brown with a greenish cast. Where there was water, white specks of herons flew below. A little farther north, drowsing on its low bluff overlooking the Mekong, was Vientiane: a scattering of houses on stilts among groves of mango and banana trees, coconut palms, bamboo, and feathery green flamboyants. Everywhere there were pagodas with upswept eaves.

We bumped to a stop in a field surrounded by other fields. There was a cluster of impromptu sheds at one end, and when I asked the way to customs and immigration, people laughed. Wells Klein hitched a ride in somebody's jeep, and we rode in through the wandering water buffaloes and the creaking high-wheeled oxcarts until the country road turned into a village street under an arcade of flowering trees.

Vientiane is a wandering village and a few lines of weathered, one-story wooden shops selling pressure lamps, cotton goods, tinned French delicacies, and a scattering of notions. Here and there on one of the three parallel main streets which make up the center of town there are a few two-story buildings. Most of the houses are built of wood and thatch and plaited bamboo, on stilts high off the ground, set back in clumps of thin bamboo and pale-green, oar-bladed banana trees. Everywhere there are pagodas. In the streets there are chickens and questing small black pigs, angular and with heads like wild boar. There are a number of pedicabs but few automobiles. This is the capital of Laos, Vientiane, the Place of Sandalwood.

Wells installed me in a long, screened bungalow, also on stilts, which was the home of Alex Moore, the Deputy Director of USOM, the American economic mission in Laos, and also it was the whole of the mission. Mr. Moore, a boyish-looking individual with a prematurely gray crew cut and an excellent command of Parisian argot, gave me a cot for a nap while Wells went out in search of the government. This was not as easy as it sounds, but after a bit he managed to track down the officials who had promised us a room at the one hotel in town, to get it back from the other people to whom it had been assigned, and to locate and introduce me to most of the officers with whom I would be working. He took me to meet the Prince Souvanna Phouma, a compact, courtly gentleman with busy black eyes who was obviously a man of great capacity. He alternated with Katay Don Sasorith as Prime Minister, and had been in office a couple of months before, signing the government's agreement with

CARE. Wells and I jolted over to the Thai river town of Nong Khai on the opposite bank, where our packages were due to arrive, and there he satisfied himself that storage facilities were adequate and everything was in order. Then he left me in my new room at the hotel, and took off for Saigon, adding hospitably that I might come down whenever things got too tough.

The hotel was called The Bungalow, or, more formally, the Settha Palace, and it seemed to grow out of the luxuriant green landscape, a long, gabled two-story building with moss growing on its tiled roof, two handsome great flamboyant trees whose parasols spread across the façade, and at the left-hand side, a little geometric garden outlined in upended wine and beer bottles. It had been the old French colonial government's guest house, and now had crumbled into a state of almost theatrical decay. It seemed always to be siesta time, with the overhead fans motionless and only the flies about in the high-ceilinged tropical dining room whose French doors gave out on the front approaches. On the tramped earth behind the hotel, beside the row of cubicles that were the kitchens and the servants' quarters, there was a woven bamboo chicken coop, a broken toilet bowl leaning against a blasted, fallen tree trunk, and a mound of approximately two thousand wine bottles.

Inside, bath and toilet facilities were of the sketchiest. My room, which was graced with a small balcony over the entrance to the building, was large and moldering. From the high ceiling at the end of a long rod hung a fan which wobbled until it seemed sure it would crash through my bed's canopy of mosquito netting. Chunks of the ceiling did crash to the floor at intervals.

I had been in worse hotels. I tried to cheer myself by remembering the Grand Hôtel des Palmistes in Cayenne in the old days when trunks and bags were carted upstairs by the living skeletons of prisoners from Devil's Island, or a place at the end of the line in Matto Grosso at Porto Esperança, Port Hope, where the lodging house had had no guests for five months, and was leaning forward into a swamp in which floated a dead boa constrictor. But it was no use. I had survived French Guiana and the Congo with reasonable cheer, but as I looked around the Settha Palace the day after Wells Klein left, I never felt quite so far away from everyone and everything I knew.

4 MORE ABOUT VIENTIANE

THE character, the flavor of Vientiane was elusive, but in the next few days I learned a little more about it. In this land of villages, Vientiane itself was essentially a collection of related villages with a total population of twenty-five or thirty thousand, with perhaps fifteen thousand more living in the town at the center. The small boys who rode the water buffaloes wore Olympic T shirts. On the naked limbs of a tree on the riverbank outside the temporary American Legation, later to become the ambassador's residence, I counted an even seventy buzzards one day, sitting there, waiting. Later I learned there was a slaughterhouse next door. In the new National Bank, a little farther along the same street, the managing director's laundry sometimes hung out to dry on a line next to the reception room.

It was tranquillity just this side of Rip Van Winkle. But there were occasional reminders of the outside world: the earthwork defenses along the roads outside the capital, the rolls of barbed wire being unloaded from barges in the Mekong, late of course, and months after the fighting was all over. The sapling that grew out of the dusty, broken brick sidewalk (one of the few bits of sidewalk in town) in front of the Vietnamese cookshop I passed every day was protected by a little circular fence also made of barbed wire, was there every morning to remind me that things can go wrong. Then, early one day as I was turning from the road into a driveway, a culvert collapsed underfoot, and I cut my shin on the gutter. This took several weeks to heal, and led me to the rambling French military hospital, Maoshot, across from the great pagoda Phra Kéo. The head of the hospital, Colonel Genêt, remarked as he fixed my leg that during the past month he had performed twenty-eight operations, most of them from people stepping on land mines.

Colonel Genêt, a spare, elegant, courtly, and balding man who had run a field hospital at Haiphong during the cruelest days of the war in North Vietnam, worked hard in this lotus land, and was himself, with his military medical colleagues in Vientiane and Luangprabang, perhaps half a dozen in all, living disproof of the old canard that there was only one doctor in all the Kingdom of Laos. It was just that there was as yet only one full-fledged Lao doctor, and he was the Minister of Public Health, of Information, and of Propaganda. There were also about a dozen Lao *médecins indochinois,* trained under the old colonial system and often enough little more than glorified dressers and compounders.

In other years, said Dr. Genêt, the Lao had usually had enough rice to eat; but there were deficiency diseases, mainly caused by lack of protein, which ended in pellagra and beri-beri. He estimated infant mortality at somewhere between thirty and forty per cent—nobody knew. He explained that the most dangerous time came when a child was weaned (it might be three or four years old if no younger brother or sister appeared), when it went straight from milk to an adult diet including chili peppers, fish sauce, and all the rest. "Dog sausage," said Dr. Genêt, resignedly.

Like so many others in bad shape, the Lao looked quite cheerful. Once I saw a young woman with no nose (yaws?) walking along the road in Vientiane on her way home from market, but she was chatting easily with a friend. All the other people I ran into seemed fine, with few outward marks, to the nonmedical eye, of the fevers and the parasites and the deficiencies that undoubtedly intensified the dreaminess and passivity for which the Lao were remarkable even three hundred years ago when Governor van Diemen of the Netherlands East Indies sent a small company of merchants from Batavia to set up an import-export business. Nothing much came of this except that the Dutchmen with tall hats like Father Knickerbocker's survive on a carved pagoda doorway in Luangprabang. But the travelers agreed with the other lone visitor of their time, the Jesuit missionary Pere de Leria, that the people were "never quarrelsome nor stubborn . . . most affable . . . docile . . . pacific . . . great friends of repose and of peace."

The Lao seem to have changed little. They call their country the Land of the Million Elephants and the White Parasol, and except for a few small inconveniences, it surely is one of the most appealing nations in this world. If the Lao are unambitious, nonmechanical, and somewhat less than miraculous at organization, they have a host of virtues: they are, above all, gentle and courteous. They are a smiling, whimsical people with a great love of parties, especially outdoor pagoda parties which are rather like church suppers with a dash of state fair. They are devout but cheerful about their religion, and have an irrepressible enthusiasm for decoration.

The Lao charm which has held the French in thrall for three generations, grandfather to grandson, seems to be a blend of shyness, beauty, simplicity, and drowsiness that fits the French Romantic tradition which began with the Noble Savage of Jean-Jacques Rousseau, reached some sort of height or depth with Chateaubriand's classic *Paul et Virginie* (in which the heroine, untrammeled by civilization, goes to her watery grave off the coast of Madagascar because she refuses to take off her outer garments before the crude sailors of her sinking ship, and swim ashore).

This is a rather one-sided, if appreciative, view of life. The Lao aren't really that silly. But they are very far from the Métro of Paris and the supermarkets of the New York suburbs. They are pacific and soft-spoken, far more interested in decorating things with curlicues than in getting ahead in the world. In Laos the Americans and their allies are faced with the problem of trying to instill a sense of economic and political urgency in a group of people who may well be the least urgent souls on earth.

Everything in Laos seems peaceful and nicely curly: the roof tops and the lottery tickets, the long serpent balustrades that lead up to the pagodas, the water buffaloes' horns and the carts the beasts pull, the heavy flatirons with the curlicue cast-iron roosters sitting on them, and the Lao language itself. On a typewriter keyboard, the symbols @ and ? are the most Lao-looking things I can find.

American impatience to get things done—our combination national virtue and drawback—is due for a workout in Laos where the two first phrases a foreigner learns are *bo mi,* or "there isn't any," and *bo pen nyan,* which can mean "never mind," "too bad," "it doesn't matter," "who cares," and a dozen other things, all gently negative. *Bo pen nyan* can make *mañana* sound dynamic. In Gallicized Lao circles, *bo mi* and *bo pen nyan* are neatly complimentary to *panné,* or "busted," and to *en principe,* a usefully vague phrase which has made its way into English in recent years. There is also, from the antiseptic, Nordic point of view, a certain insouciant Franco-Lao agreement as to what constitutes hygiene and sanitation. All this adds to the feckless charm baffling to the transplanted American under pressure and in a hurry.

The American population in Vientiane at first fluctuated between perhaps ten and twenty, and I found myself constituting twenty-five per cent of the nonofficial or civilian American population of the capital, and one hundred per cent of the nonofficial, nonclerical American population. The other civilians were Protestant and Catholic missionaries, cheerfully evangelizing after many years and very few converts among the Buddhists. They had recorded sermons in Lao. At one time seventy-eight per cent of the American population was Princetonian. I can think of no use at all for this statistic, except perhaps that I should have sent it in to the *Princeton Alumni Weekly.*

A few weeks before, the entire American economic mission in Laos had consisted of one woman, Nan McKay, whom I'd met in Saigon just as she finished her tour. For a long time the whole outfit was known to Vientiane's small switchboard as "Maison Miss McKay," since it was in her long bungalow on stilts that the telephone was located. Now, Carter de Paul, an economist who had been a professor at Brown, and Alex Moore, as his deputy, had moved their expanding force into an olive-green office tent in the garden of the Minister's house. It was the influx of clerks and stenographers and junior officers brought in to cope with the mounting paper work in the embassy and USOM that provided the most remarkable contrasts between the Lao and the American Ways of Life.

The American Minister, Charles Woodruff Yost, was a quiet, slender, bookish, perceptive, and sometimes slightly unexpected man who, as a student, had once been to the Parisian Bal des Quat'z'Arts as a South Sea Islander dressed in a flap of burlap. He was known from time to time in the rather porous, bisque-colored, mimeographed daily *Lao-Presse* as Sir YOST. His chief was Sir John Foster DULLES, or Sir DULLES. In a few months time, when Sir DULLES was able to make a day's stopover in Vientiane, and the American colony had grown to a few dozens—perhaps fifty—he was so staggered by what he saw that he topped the observation of Representative Patrick J. Billings of California that the United States Embassy in Moscow was "like a pigpen" with the comment that Congressman Billings ought to see Vientiane. Mr. Dulles, according to the New York *Times*, "spoke feelingly of . . . women secretaries and clerks living in primitive housing without sanitary facilities," and said that the Vientiane Embassy contained "no plumbing." Mr. Dulles was drawing a long bow; things weren't really quite as bad as that. But the initial shock of an uprooted American suddenly finding himself in Vientiane, at the end of the line, was considerable. The reaction of the Lao themselves to the superficial Americanization of Vientiane was more sophisticated: they certainly gave no sign of being disturbed at all by these outlanders piling in on top of them, and a good deal of the time they didn't even appear to be aware of them.

It was fortunate that Mr. Dulles and his entourage were not billeted at The Bungalow, where the American Embassy maintained a couple of rooms. The hotel offered an almost unparalleled opportunity for us to prove that the American frontier tradition was not dead.

There was a dying praying mantis on the floor when I was shown into the barnlike room which was to be the CARE office and my home off and on for most of the next year, and in the bottom of the night table were a hypodermic syringe and three rusty needles wrapped in a Siamese newspaper. The mosquito nets over the twin double beds in the room looked as though they had been dipped in tea, and were punctured with holes, some of which were sewn up or tied with bits of string. A three-bladed ceiling fan revolved slowly at the end of a long wobbling pole, and from the fan hung a naked, unfrosted electric light bulb. But the French doors that opened onto the room's little balcony gave out on a canopy of green leaves, epiphytes and creepers on the ancient tree trunks, and beyond them, on the other side of the road, buffaloes browsing peacefully, and a couple of sporting Lao playing ping-pong on a table they had set up in the pasture. Off to one side could be heard the high whining buzz of the world's smallest sawmill.

After lunch there were piles of laundry on the tiles of the corridors. This was the quiet time, for everyone was asleep or had left the building. The room boys curled up like a basket of puppies on an extra double bed with mosquito net frame in the hall. When they were awake, and if one could find them, the management and the staff were friendly and accommodating, although they had their own way of dealing with the intrusions of the technological West. I have seen four youthful members of the staff, on duty, gazing motionless but with interest at the hotel's telephone ringing and ringing on the bar. Since the staff to a man sensibly went home at eleven o'clock on most nights, guests returning later were greeted by locked and bolted doors; they found it easier not to complain, but to break in through the dining-room windows.

Downstairs a door marked "WC" led to a broom closet filled with cobwebs. There was a second telephone just at the right of the entrance connected with the Dove exchange operated by the Indian Signal Corps of the International Control Commission. Copies of *The Hindu* and the *Times of India* were scattered among the *Lao-Presse* and the ICC communiqués on the coffee tables in the foyer. In the smaller dining room to the right, there were trim, military Sikhs, as usual with turbans and beard nets; newly arrived Poles looking a little pale and uncomfortable in their first tropical whites; smart young Canadian officers with swagger sticks. They were a richly varied crew. I met a Hindu wing commander who was also a child psychiatrist, and a French-English translator from Geneva who was part Russian, part Arab, and who had the exquisite, ironic manner of a Restoration fop. The man from the semiofficial Agence Franco-Presse, who ran the *Lao-Presse* under contract and who lived down the hall, and I were about the only non-ICC people among the hotel's permanent faithful lodgers. We were lucky. There were many others, though few if any Americans, who were eager to become permanent faithful lodgers, but there was never any room, and you had to watch your bed like a hawk or someone would promote your accommodation out from under you. On one trip back to Vientiane from upcountry, dusty and unwashed, wearing the same clothes I had been sleeping in for several days during a food distribution in the famine area, I found blue and yellow underclothes hung on my balcony, the door locked, and the premises occupied by a lady photographer from a picture magazine who stayed put for three days while I scrounged a place to sleep elsewhere.

From the taps in the hotel came a tawny stream of Mekong water and gradually all the bath towels and white clothes turned a rich old-ivory color. The water was rich in iron, too, and after a while, left black streaks on one's teeth. On wet nights there were invasions of mole crickets, tiger beetles, giant scarabs, and more praying mantises. At some seasons there were invasions of flies so that guests in the bar in white suits looked as though they were studded with raisins. Mosquitoes were pesky and plentiful, but most of them didn't even bite very hard, and there were few anopheles around Vientiane, so there wasn't much malaria.

In the dining room off the bar the boarders grappled with the table d'hôte. *Toujours poulet.* There were the quick, friendly, passionately intellectual young Frenchmen and French women, fresh from Paris, who taught at the *lycée.* There were the Air Laos pilots at dinner with their families after the daily routine of flying over the southern savannahs and the misty northern mountains, where the maps were sometimes a good twelve degrees, or about fifty miles, off in the region of the Chinese and North Vietnamese frontiers. They knit together a sprawling country whose roads were impassable, ran a biweekly service for the ICC from Hanoi in the Communist north of Vietnam through Vientiane and Phnom-Penh to Saigon in the south, and with a couple of helicopter pilots from the French Army, were the only non-ICC people to hop back and forth between the government-held fields and the Pathet Lao strongholds in the two most northerly provinces of Samneua and Phongsaly. They would fly anything anywhere, except possibly opium, though most of them had been approached at one time or another by the traffickers who seemed to run a thriving export business right through the Bamboo Curtain. Their flying had something of the dash of a boy's adventure story. They could make up to fifteen hundred dollars a month—more than that when there was a shooting war on—but they earned it, for the job was hazardous in many ways. One night a pilot named Catry with whom we worked came into The Bungalow dining room visibly shaken: after landing a Pathet Lao officer at the rustic Communist capital of Samneua, complete with a wickerwork peace arch and wickerwork Picasso doves, the officer had disappeared, whereupon Catry had been captured by some youthful comrades who marched him off into the woods, tied him to a tree, and had begun jumping around him excitedly, poking him in the ribs with a submachine gun. Catry was eventually identified and extricated by his passenger, but he didn't enjoy the afternoon. There were many such stories, but father usually got home in time for dinner with his wife while their children played up and down the dining room in a highly un-Anglo-Saxon manner, but one well adapted to Laos.

The new Prime Minister, Katay Don Sasorith, who sometimes wore his badge of office pinned to his sweater vest, was fond of entertaining other convivial dignitaries at banquets in the main dining room, and on these occasions the Vietnamese chef did his best to produce a meal that at least looked on paper like French *haute cuisine*. On New Year's Eve, the manager of the hotel, a very sensitive, very kindly, and very nervous man, offered his guests cold consommé with port, rabbit roasted with prunes, asparagus vinaigrette, goose with truffles and potato chips, endive salad, Brie and Camembert, custard in liqueur, and coffee. It really was quite good, with lashings of wine and champagne. Perhaps I was carried away by New Year's Eve, but for a few weeks I didn't get around to eating at Dirty Dan's up the street. Both restaurants were dirty, both were expensive (white beans, 86 cents a portion), But Dan had a better cook. Meanwhile, I tried to come to terms with my new environment: if one ignored the falling plaster, one could study at siesta time the free-form, tabletop-sized patches of naked lath in the ceiling as a nonobjective composition. Approach the matter as an old campaigner. Keep a couple of buckets of water in the shower in expectation of a daily breakdown of the water supply; keep a battery of large candles and two flashlights (one for lending) for all the nights the lights go out; make sure the bottles of drinking water are filtered and corked; avoid using the community toilet except around noon when it has just been cleaned; and keep a good stock of insecticide and antimalarial prophylactic. Learn to shave by sense of touch, and if necessary, bathe in a glass of water. Use an empty carton for a wastebasket, and cigarette tins for ash trays. And in the case of The Bungalow, never lock your room or put your money in the hotel strong-box, or someone will wander off with the keys, and there you are.

It all took a little time to get used to. One day shortly after I had arrived, a few minutes before my first meeting with the Prime Minister, I found myself among the rubble and the dovecotes and the piles of empty bottles in the back yard of the hotel, naked to the waist and almost incoherent with rage and alarm, crying that the shirts which were supposed to have been washed over a week ago still weren't back.

The hotel manager said sadly, "You are too exigent, monsieur. You must be more supple."

"What happened to that one-day service?"

"You cannot be too rigid, monsieur. You must be more supple."

Gradually one became aware of the other side of it. The hotel was plagued with the problem of replacing servants, gentle Lao who were so unhappy if rebuffed by one of the guests that they could not stay. Foreign hotel promoters who began to turn up in some numbers, visibly excited by tales of the wide-open Vientiane market and all the American money in town, took one look around and began to talk quickly about importing complete staffs from Hong Kong.

At first it is all very exasperating and sometimes frustrating. But somehow, a surprising number of times it comes out all right in the end. If you are stranded in the hinterland and fail to get back to town in time for an important appointment with somebody, it may well be that he wasn't there anyway. And if the driver to take you to the airfield is an hour late, it is quite possible that the take-off will be an hour late, too.

"When things go wrong," an old Lao hand told me, "we Europeans and Americans take a combative attitude and try to redress the situation. But the Lao attitude is to withdraw, like a hedgehog. Because he is a Buddhist, he has been taught resignation, passivity, and to hope that the catastrophe will pass over."

It is not long before the newcomer is enmeshed in the Lao Way of Life. I used to stand on the balcony in the early morning watching the women carrying over one shoulder flat, tapered bamboo strips hung with baskets, babies, vegetables, and little low rattan stools and tables, which they would set up in the open-air market place in front of USIS, the United States Information Service, beside the bicycle and pedicab stands in the middle of town. Lao have broad shoulders and sturdy legs, and the older women—in their thirties or so, and past all worldly vanity—wear their gray hair in a short crew-cut shock that makes them look a little like William Faulkner. The young girls wear their hair pulled back and tied a little to one side in a high chignon and, on special occasions, circled with an antique gold chain and stuck with a great gold hatpin. They can be seen on these days cycling to a party or a pagoda, carrying a *repoussé* silver bowl filled with flowers or incense or other offerings, wearing an embroidered Lao shawl instead of, or as well as, the latter-day blouse, and around their improbably slender waists, elegant openwork belts of gold or silver. The skirt is always the *sin*, a cotton or silk sarong that falls just below the calf, usually with a dark, small-figured pattern, subtly handsome, and at its most elegant, bordered with embroidered bands of gold and silver cloth or a wide harlequin strip of gold and green and orange red.

Many of the women, like the Chinese, are a little bald in the manner of Queen Elizabeth I, with a high forehead and irregular, receding hairline. But they are lovely, with oval faces, high cheekbones, and a quiet, almost detached sort of beauty. They laugh together as they walk along, and they look straight at strangers with an interested smile, yet they are shy.

Both men and women seem simple and direct, and both are modest. Women nurse their babies in public, but with great delicacy; when they bathe in the Mekong, they wash themselves and their clothes at the same time, hitching their sarongs up under their arms. Men use the short, black-and-white-checked, kilt-like sarong rather like a bistro tablecloth as a bathing costume, towel, washcloth, and turban. Most people still wear the sarong at home for sleep and siesta, but standard dress for the male has become, at least in the capital and large towns, the usual nondescript Western shirt and pants, sometimes topped with a felt hat.

It was frosty at Christmas in Vientiane, like fall football weather in New England, and the early morning curtain of mist half shrouded the figures walking in the road in front of my balcony, the big gray and white ganders with knobs on their heads and a dignified waddle across the way, and the leisurely pedicab pedaling someone to market. Later, as the sun came up, the haze lifted, the meadows and ponds and flotillas of ducks became more distinct, and as the heat of the day took strength, the boy bonzes appeared with lacquered parasols instead of the begging bowls with which they had earlier collected their food. With a clacking of two sticks of wood like the *claves* in a Cuban rumba band, the first Chinese soup wagon appeared on the road, like an old-fashioned ice-cream cart with a little roof and under it a row of bottles of soy sauce, fish sauce, vinegar, and poison-pink and electric-green soda pop, and at one side a cage of wire screening in which hung a chunk of water buffalo beef, a bundle of assorted greens, and a cluster of scallions hung by their white heads. In the center of the top of the cart was a big round brass lid covering a suspended pot of hot water and one of soup stock simmering over a charcoal fire at the center of the cart. A few cents produced a bowl of succulent broth crowded with a tangle of freshly cooked noodles, thin strips of beef, chopped scallions, chili peppers, and coriander leaves like a fusty parsley—*soupe chinoise* to the French, simply noodles to the Chinese—eaten with chopsticks and a Chinese spoon, and just the thing on a crisp winter's morning.

Later in the day there would be small white herons suddenly flapping through the cool green arcade of the road next door that led between the rice fields and clumps of papayas and bananas, past the small streams and copses, and a great, open-sided market whose eaves were enlivened by brilliant polychrome reliefs of demons and heros from the *Ramayana*. There were few cats but dogs everywhere, and at high noon, metallic green-and-blue flies buzzing over the mango pits on the road. There was no line between town and country, any more than there was between Sunday (or anybody else's sabbath) and weekdays.

Vientiane had the flavor of a frontier town, with the usual expensive importations. The two or three jerry-built two-story brick buildings in bamboo scaffolding beginning to appear in the center of town were flanked by rows of Indian merchants selling saris and gents' natty suiting, Chinese shops stocked with Roy Rogers T shirts, Lucky Dollar Calmex abalone, photomontage novelty shirts covered with American newspaper headlines or advertisements, and tinned *pâté de foie gras*. One item which they stocked was a fine example of that sort of cultural ping-pong which Professor Herskovits likes to call transculturation: a dark-brown Siamese sauce called Maggic which was an imitation of an Anglo-French sauce called Maggi which was in turn an imitation of the old original Chinese soy sauce.

Every once in a while one can see a member of the Lao Navy, the Mekong river patrol, who wear French uniforms with the brimless white sailor's cap and the red pom-pom on top; they look well on the Lao sailors, especially with their own squiggly writing in gold on the band. Military medals are imported, too, their marvelously elaborate three-headed elephant and Buddhist battalion devices all enameled and gilded in Paris. There have been attempts to pull up Vientiane's municipal socks, to impose European standards, but they usually end up with a slight Lao flavor, like the marker at the edge of town on the way to the airport which was broadminded enough to report Luangprabang 306 kilometers on one side and Luangprabang 307 kilometers on the other.

Somehow—and it used to remind me of the way that English has managed to borrow words from French and Chinese, Polynesian and Russian, and make them its own—things foreign in this country were infused with a Lao-ness which made them subtly a part of the national culture. A really good servant spoke in a sort of French, but he put his hands on his knees when he did so. I once followed the strains of wild, weird Oriental music on a hot midday in The Bungalow, and found a man behind the bar sitting on the floor and playing Lao tunes on a banjo.

One day in a village near Vientiane, Nivong, the Lao government's Social Welfare officer, spilled a few drops on the ground from a bottle of drinking water on the table in a roadside noodle shop where we were taking lunch.

"What's that? A libation for the gods?" I asked, happy in my anthropological background reading.

"No, just to get the dust off the top," said Nivong.

I still had a lot to learn.

5 LOGISTICS IN DREAMLAND

NIVONG SOUVANNAHEUNG was square-cut, jolly, with a shock of hair like a brush. A permanent civil servant in Laos' budding bureaucracy, he was attached to the Department of Social Welfare, directly under the Prime Minister, and lived with his wife, the kingdom's first qualified midwife, in a traditional thatched house on stilts in the middle of a bosky block near the river and just behind the Thai Embassy. Mme Nivong was ample and also jolly, and she found time to command a bevy of Lao girls who looked after the wives and children of Lao army men, and who periodically visited troops in the field to cheer them up and bring them a breath of life in the metropolis.

Nivong was from Xiengkhouang, a provincial center to the northeast where he had taken to the woods and worked with the French, British, and American underground during the Second World War. He loved to tell ghost stories and stories about the resistance, and was fine company, but he was especially valuable because he was reliable in an unraveled world. I lost one of his predecessors—nameless and unprintable— earlier drafted to serve as liaison man between the government and CARE when he wrote himself orders to *"perfectionner la liaison CARE à Saïgon,"* and took off for a few weeks' tour of the Vietnamese shops and dance halls.

Fifteen thousand packages of food—rice, beans, shortening, butter, and cheese, mostly American surplus stocks donated by the US Department of Agriculture and sent on their way by fifteen thousand people at home who gave a dollar each to get them to Laos—were supposed to be landed at Bangkok and come overland on the Thai railway which ended at Udorn, a few miles short of the Lao border, and arrive in Vientiane early in the new year. Then it should be a simple matter to send the packages a couple of miles by truck to the Mekong and a few miles upriver to Vientiane. It looked fine: the bold red railway line on the map reached almost to Vientiane; the Thai government was kind enough to say that its Express Transport Bureau would carry the packages free as its contribution; everyone in Vientiane concerned with customs, transport, and so on assured us there would be no trouble. The only trouble was that nobody knew where Vientiane was. This was borne in on me slowly as I waited for money to arrive. From the Chase National Bank in New York to the Banque Nationale d'Indo-Chine in Vientiane, then the only bank in town, the first draft took six weeks and two days by cable.

Nivong found a jeep for me, part of the government transport pool, an old jeep with its broken right door fastened with a lady's pink garter. In it I shuttled around town, out to the airport, down to the landing stage, around to the various government offices to discover if anyone had heard of our packages arriving somehow without my having heard of it, and to the warehouse in the hospital grounds to make sure no one had yet sneaked into the space we had been promised for storage. It was important to keep an eye on the jeep, too. Transport of any sort was at a premium, and there was never enough to go around for the few government people who needed it. One day I discovered my borrowed jeep commandeered for a delegation of the Pathet Lao. Later it disappeared altogether, and I pedaled up and down the bank of the Mekong by the local pedicab, familiarly known as the *pousse-pousse*, or push-push.

In order to tell the pedicab drivers which way to go, I bought a copy of the only dictionary available in town, the *Lexique Franco-Laotien à l'Usage des Élèves Infirmiers,* which had a general vocabulary of some eighteen hundred words, plus handy lists of diseases, symptoms, medicines, parts of the body, and a final glossary of sixty-one useful phrases in Lao which seemed a touch professional for everyday use:

> Cough, please.
> I can't breathe.
> Are you perspiring?
> Have you had any false pregnancies?
> You will have to bottle-feed.
> You'll get better soon.
> You'll have to have an operation.

Everyday we pedaled about town to see if there were any news. Then, finally, one day the packages came. The Prime Minister, accompanied by Laos' only motorcycle outriders, with sirens, green berets, and wide white belts, roared down with a party of "personages" to welcome them at the landing stage at Kilometre 4. The captain of the *Peng Hong*, a tug-boat ornamented with little red-and-blue scallops, and of its two freight sampans which had carried our supplies from Nong Khai, the river port closest to the railroad on the Thai side, promised as soon as he finished unloading that he would surely let me have the brief Vessel Outturn Report form which I was expected to send immediately to CARE in New York with details of the number of packages arriving in good condition, damaged, pilfered, or missing. I had been impressed with the importance of supplying information promptly; CARE carried insurance on some tens of millions of dollars' worth of cargo, and was obligated to deliver it.

To begin with we had a relatively small share in Laos. But still, it was more than 150 tons of food. When it was all safely stacked in the hospital storehouse, and when all seemed to be in order, I had dinner and went to bed, much relieved. That night, between eleven-thirty and twelve-thirty—and this made it extremely difficult to assign a day to the insurance claims—the tugboat captain took off for Thailand, with no report as to how many boxes he believed he had delivered.

That was Saturday night. News reached me just as I thought I was about to enjoy a quiet Sunday breakfast. Offices were closed, but I managed to find Nivong, and he found a jeep and the two giggling Social Welfare secretaries (one as chaperone) and off we went, bucketing the twenty-nine kilometers down the country road to Thadeua, a village on the bluffs of the Mekong where passengers scrambled down a steep sort of goat path, over the roots of the great buttressed trees that grew on the riverbank and sheltered the village, and to one of the flotilla of Thai and Lao launches, small, weathered craft which looked as though they had been made a long time ago in a manual training class and which sometimes drifted quite a way downstream when the motor stopped and refused to start again. In a fit of modernization the Thai some years ago had removed the large white elephant from their horizontally striped red, white, and blue flag, so that it now looked like a good many other national flags, but the Lao three-headed white elephant on a scarlet field still snapped bravely from the Lao jackstaffs.

On the Thai side we scrambled up another steep bank and found ourselves in Nong Khai. There were more pagodas and monks in orange robes, more Chinese soup wagons and little shops, with gold and lacquer Chinese signs, crowded with hardware, plastic novelties, dried codfish like shingles, split and glazed dried ducks and chickens, cheap printed cottons and shimmering Thai and Lao silks. There were also more soldiers in sand-colored khaki; in the shops patriotic lithographs of the bespectacled, serious young Thai King. There were gaudily painted pedicabs whose drivers wore straw sun helmets; Thai schoolgirls, straight black hair chopped in a 1920s bob, going home in little gaggles in the street laughing were charming, swinging their schoolbooks; dressed in navy-blue pleated skirts, white middy blouses with blue kerchief, and chalked white sun helmets (the free and independent Thai seemed to love colonial helmets). But there was no tugboat captain in sight, and no one had heard of our fifteen thousand packages which had just been carried through town.

Armed with the Vessel Outturn Reports, I jumped on a bus for Udorn, about fifty kilometers down the pike, and the end of the railway from Bangkok where our supplies had been transshipped. It was a wonderful, rattling, banging, bouncing trip, like traveling inside an electric vibrator, and at forty miles an hour down the red laterite road it seemed suicidally swift when we passed another bulging, careering, careening bus, caroming off the other side of the road coming toward us, or hurtling at a narrow bridge full throttle. There were more small brown boys riding charcoal-gray water buffaloes in the green paddy fields here, and white water birds like egrets which picked insects from the buffaloes and cattle. But the fields and the yards in front of the houses on stilts looked neater than on the other side of the river. Also, we had to stop every so often at a police control point, which was very un-Lao; this was part of the country settled by pro-Vietminh refugees from Vietnam, in villages still tightly controlled by their own Communist constabulary and rural courts.

All I learned in the railhead and provincial center of Udorn was that the people responsible for the Udorn-Nong Khai-Vientiane link in the shipment were at the moment in Nong Khai. Back to Nong Khai, and to a Chinese merchant's on the main street where the most important person seemed to be an agreeable old lady sitting beside a white-and-red-flowered enameled spittoon, chewing betel. Eventually a couple of subordinate shippers were produced, both apparently playing hookey from school. They agreed that it would be impossible for the shipping company to say, on paper, how many packages it thought it had landed in Vientiane, or in what condition. With the help of Nang (Mlle) Lanoy Souvannavong and Nang Bounxam Sananikone, and eloquent pleas in English, French, Lao, and Thai, the shippers were finally persuaded to sign our own count of what had arrived. The Vessel Outturn Report was complete. Laden with Nang Lanoy's and Nang Bounxam's Cutex nail varnish and other trophies of our visit to Thailand, we made the laborious, weary, triumphant return by pedicab, foot, launch, and jeep back to Vientiane.

Later I realized how lucky we were to have made it in a single day.

Back in Laos, I checked the warehouse next morning to see that all was in order and found the place locked up, with nobody in sight, and a hand-lettered notice in English tacked to the door:

> Date 15th January B.E. 1955
> Dont 6pen the door.
> When he is not the Mogaryang.
> Because it has not time and when he come
> he 6pen the door.
> "Short the door."
> "Bengyong."

I still don't know what it means.

6 THE HONG AND THE WILD BLUE YONDER

DURING the monsoon, until recently, it was impossible to go by car from the capital province of Vientiane to any of the other eleven Lao provinces. Just before I left the country the road between the government capital of Vientiane and the royal capital of Luangprabang was supposed to be restored, but about the same time, the deputy director of the American aid mission was celebrated for having been able to get halfway by jeep, making his own bridges and rafts to cross the streams as he went.

A good part of the Mekong in Laos is navigable only during the rainy season, and most of the country is served by trails and shallow waterways. But Air Laos, the small but lively national airline which has taken as its symbol the curly mythological bird called the *hong*, flies to village airfields at the main provincial centers, and there are still in business a number of the little charter outfits which proliferated during the

Indochinese war, flying supplies to Dienbienphu, a few miles beyond the northeastern Lao frontier. The planes are American or British or Canadian, but the pilots and navigators are French. Some of them have been flying by the seat of their pants through this indifferently mapped country for almost ten years. There had been a couple of DC-3 crashes just before I arrived, one of which killed Henri Deydier of the École Française d'Extrême-Orient, probably the best known of the anthropologists working in Laos. Still, one must get around somehow, and the planes are a partial solution to the cargo bottleneck.

There were the usual confusions and delays and frustrations which seem inevitable in trying to meet a deadline in these latitudes, but somehow the truckloads of food packages moved from the hospital storehouse out to the Vientiane airfield near the pagoda Vat Tay. Most of the packages were carried out to the provincial centers by that old workhorse, the DC-3 with the *hong*, curly as a firebird, on its nose if it were from Air Laos, or the three-headed elephant under its parasols on those occasions when we got a helping hand from the Lao Army. Air Laos also had a couple of Bristol Wayfarers, big-bellied planes suggestive of a pregnant whale, whose noses could open to swallow up a large truck. A modification of a wartime transport glider, the Bristol carried its pod-like engines suspended from wings above the fat fuselage, and the pilot high up in the nose. Those of us who were sitting on the sea of cargo in the Bristol's belly, feet braced against the CARE packages ahead of us to keep from pitching forward, were a deck below and somewhat aft of him. A metal ladder ran from the cockpit down into the hold, and cables led from the cockpit over our heads to work the ailerons behind us. These kept creaking, and the engines made such an infernal racket in this echo chamber that one fine day I lost my voice completely after trying to shout a CARE report into the ear of Jane Lau, on loan from Saigon, who was seated, demure and imperturbable with her stenographer's notebook, on a stack of food packages. There were sometimes a couple of seats bolted to the back of the Bristols, and often a few more on the DC-3s, but we learned the futility of complaining at some far-off airstrip when a plane turned up with two seats for three people, or with four seats boasting between them: one with a regulation safety belt, one with half a safety belt, one with no safety belt, and one with two left sides to a safety belt. We picked up the technique of sitting in the rear of the plane (a little safer) and holding the strap or bar overhead. There had been too many accidents.

Wells Klein, also borrowed from Saigon, and I hitched a ride on one of the military DC-3s to see how some of the first distributions were going in the Vietminh-devastated area just to the north of Luangprabang. Our fellow hitchhikers were boy bonzes in their orange robes and cloth shoulder bags, nursing mothers, and government officials. There was an overhead wire for paratroops leading to the door, and other military touches like the stretchers secured against the bulkhead, a washroom urinal whose basin was covered with the dust of ages, and the outlets marked "Troop Oxygen." There were also, in the side of the plane, a couple of fair-sized holes leading to outer space. A captain returning to duty in the north was sleeping on top of a pile of bags of grain as we took off, and a number of youthful parachutists, wearing camouflage battle dress and cherry-colored berets with ribbons, grinned as we passed a flock of vultures picking at a water buffalo carcass beside the runway. The French crew had three bottles of Algerian wine up forward. When we tucked down at Luangprabang, coming in over the river, with the high mountains ringing us all around, there were a row of tanks parked off to one side and also bits of aluminum wreckage, almost overgrown with weeds and creepers, glinting in the sun.

At Luangprabang was Yale Richmond from the United States Information Service who wanted to take some pictures for the USIS magazine and their new Lao newsreel. Wells and Yale and I found a small plane called *Popeye*, a gray, canvas-covered little Norseman which would take us north to Muong Sai, where several planeloads of food had already arrived. The *Popeye* later somersaulted, killing its distinguished silver-haired pilot and two passengers, but we got through our work without any difficulty beyond a tendency to scare ourselves to death.

All three of us are congenital cowards, and we found ourselves staving off fate by making jokes. Yale was a quick, generous, sandy, medium-small fellow with a rather sharp, friendly face and rimless, tinted spectacles; he wore pale-blue denim pants, a black-and-white-checked shirt, and a leather-rimmed beret with eyelets, lacings, and ribbons at the back that made him look like a refugee from Montgomery's desert army. "I'm heavily overinsured," he said, "and since I don't have anything else to think about when the plane is taking off, I think about that."

The mountains around Luangprabang came rushing up to meet us, and we snaked our way through the misty passes. A little later, Yale leaned out of the small plane to take pictures while I held him by hanging on to his belt. There were more and more razor ridges, and cones, knobs, and spires of mountains below, with an occasional small clearing on top of a mountain that might be a Meo tribesman's family opium patch. I found myself wondering why, if we were all so un-courageous, we persisted in thrusting ourselves into such un-suitable situations. Because the job was there, I suppose, and also in great part because our curiosity proved stronger than our fear.

After a bit we bumped down on a field at Muong Sai, a mountain crossroads whose surrounding villages had been completely destroyed, twice invaded by the Vietminh, then bombed by the French in American-built planes who were chasing the Vietminh. The fields and the land around the schoolhouse were mined, so there was no farming and no school. The captain of the local forces estimated that of the invading forces he had met, perhaps eighty per cent were Vietnamese, with the remainder Chinese, Thai, and Lao. In his barracks was a crudely drawn poster of the Lao national elephant chasing a soldier in a Vietminh uniform.

There was a crowd of Meo tribesmen in the village, down from the surrounding mountains on which the Vietminh had sat and poured fire at the French and Royal Lao troops be-low, as they had done at Dienbienphu and all the other inde-fensible strongholds in that war. Indochina had been a series of Dienbienphus—airstrips and strong points in valleys ringed with commanding heights.

The Meo youths wore their hair long, and black pajama suits; Lao charms were tattooed blue-black on their brown wrists. A small boy wore a slingshot around his neck. There was a lot of laughing and horseplay when thumbprints were taken from the villagers as signatures to send back to the donors overseas. The young people's hands were smooth and tawny, the old people's gnarled with purple flecks. Most had spatulate fingernails. *"Pung! Pung! Bang! Bang!"* cried the local headman, as he handed a food package to a pretty girl.

The assistant to the provincial governor made a stirring public address, but this was Laos and he spoke so softly that one could hardly hear him.

The crews of the DC-3s ("Dakota," they called it here, after the European fashion) and the other planes in which I made my Lao rounds were an adaptable, relaxed, and good-natured crowd who regularly flew under conditions which would make the American Civil Aeronautics Board go green at the gills. The senior pilot of the national airline, a Frenchman with many years' experience in these mountains, seemed to be a trim, lean septuagenarian wearing George Washington's teeth, who held a map against his nose to read, but he took off and landed beautifully, and flew so well I felt safe enough.

Some of the airmen were now solid, balding family men in early middle years who were saving their pay against their retirement in France, but there was a certain dash in mountain and ricefield-hopping life. One of the Air Laos radio-navigators, Jerôme Moveza, had run away at sixteen from the Vichy Guadeloupe of Admiral Robert, joined the Free French Air Force, and now found himself in Indochina. He was a good, easy man on a difficult trip, and in his time off, the delight of all the dancing girls in Saigon. There was another neo-African pilot in town, an older man from the Canary Islands, who had worked his way over via jungle charter outfits in Dakar, the Ivory coast, and across Africa. The officer who cheered me most was Pettenaro, an irrepressible and highly disrespectful *radio-navigant* from Nice who spoke Niçois, and talked about the Afro-Asian world like a caricature of a nineteenth-century tropical planter but behaved with a reverse kindness and friendliness; he had happily married a Franco-Vietnamese stewardess named Jacky. He later gave a very good account of himself when, in Peking on a good-will flight with the Lao Prime Minister, their Chinese hosts had challenged the French crew to a wine-drinking contest.

There were days when we could use Pettenaro's good cheer. On one we would both like to forget, Wells Klein and I found ourselves flying back from delivering three planeloads of food in the far northwest when the captain of our DC-3 signaled the pilots on his right and left to fly wingtip to wingtip, and in close formation buzzed the villages and then the capital itself. When I pulled myself forward, hand over hand, to ask him please to be an acrobat on his own time, I got a cheery smile. He was later put out to pasture, and I felt that Laos was a lot safer.

The weeks went by, and as I rode circuit around the kingdom, trying to find proper warehousing, set up local distributions and be on hand for as many myself as was humanly possible, see that the signatures and thumbprints for all the fifteen thousand packages were returned to be sent back to New York, gradually the country began to take shape. There was the wild and rugged north, the tropical green south, the great fertile plateaus, and always the backbone of the mountains. There were a myriad variations on the theme, but everywhere were the houses on stilts, the little burnt-sienna monks in orange robes, the pagodas with the tiered, swooping roofs and the curls at the ends, the slender dugouts on the waterways, the ricefields with women and children catching small fish in baskets like parrot cages, and the contentedly sloshing water buffaloes wearing flattened horns curling up at the side like a Dutch girl's cap.

We flew over the gorges and the furry green mountains,

through the fogs and the *brume sèche,* that curious smoky haze from the fields being burned over at this time of year that turned the sun into a bloody orange. We traveled to places with romantic names like Saravane and Sayaboury, Xiengkhouang and Luangprabang.

There were dust devils spinning across the field when we reached Xiengkhouang, and lines of barbed wire around the strong points piled with sandbags at the desolate military base there. More barbed wire was piled in small fat coils, like elephant-gray wash. Here in the northeast, with the blue and dark-green mountains rising all around, it was both dustier and craggier than in the south. There was no food to be had at the rest house at the field, just a lavatory with a clear brook running swiftly through it, and a bar built on four brown wine casks, well stocked with cognac, cassis, vermouth, peppermint, Pernod, and Perrier.

On the roads were Meo down from their white poppy fields in the mountains above for the opium market nearby, light skinned, with ruddy cheeks and chipmunk eyes, wearing dark-blue turbans and great dog collars of silver; the Black Thai refugees from Dienbienphu for whom we had brought food, the women a handsome, light ivory, and wearing green jade bracelets and a long-sleeved black bodice with a high collar and a line of worked silver buckles down the front. This was all their fortune, but they were still hungry. They watched while our boxes were being unloaded, when suddenly the soldiers doing the work began throwing the twenty-one-pound boxes from the plane to the ground, roaring with laughter when they broke, scattering rice over the airstrip. I tried entreaties and threats in various languages, but it didn't do any good. It was five forty-five in the afternoon. The Xiengkhouang field closed down at six o'clock, and the field at Vientiane, a good hour away, at seven—after which, planes were supposed to circle the unlit field until their tanks were empty. We roared out of Xiengkhouang at 6:08 with the door still open.

Once I got away from the airfields, things became a little more Lao and relaxed. At a tardy breakfast one day with the governor of one of the northwestern provinces, we heard the bugler from the garrison next door blow the eight o'clock reveille at nine-thirty. But the governor just looked up from his sticky rice and hot pepper sauce, and mildly said, "Ah, late again!"

Farther south, at Seno, about halfway down the line, the French maintained their last airbase, and here was more barbed wire, fencing African troop barracks on the flat plain. The old French *bordel militaire* in Vientiane, one was told, had been moved to Seno. Beside the airfield were stored rows of stubby napalm bombs like fat cigars.

At Saravane, near the end of the line flying south, there was the ever-present barbed wire and log and sod fortifications in the classical French colonial form of a star with attenuated points. All Laos was not barbed wire; it was just that the places where CARE's food would be of most use were those which had been hardest hit. Saravane had been evacuated before it was occupied by the Vietminh armies moving in from central Vietnam the year before, but the townspeople had returned, and there were again water buffaloes wandering placidly under the houses, and once more offerings of bright paper flowers in the old pagoda with its murals of fighting elephants and balletic warrior kings in costumes like those of Balinese dancers. There was also a small hospital of sorts, with hypodermics lying on the floor and uncleaned enameled basins whose contents had been evaporating for some days; the Chinese doctor-dispenser had been away for some time, and no one seemed to know when he would be back.

On the trip to Attopeu, which was farther south and the last stop before the Vietnamese frontier, I was given one of those periodic opportunities offered to tropical travelers to demonstrate their powers of survival. The night before, after going to bed early, I woke about midnight with one of those infernal alimentary upsets known in various parts of the world as Gyppy tummy, Delhi belly, the tourist's dilemma, Montezuma's revenge, and the Aztec curse. A night of nausea, violent stomach cramps, and cold sweat was followed before dawn by an odd tightness of the throat which left me almost unable to swallow, and scared me stiff.

I was weak as a washrag in the early morning, and very nearly didn't get to the plane in time for take-off. The sun was a red nimbus in the opalescent mists, and it was a little better in the cold above the clouds, but I was listless with fatigue, and didn't get much done on the way. Then we came down into the Turkish-bath tropics, and there in the village capital of Attopeu, with a little bright-blue river winding through the rainforest green and the thatched houses on the banks and the mountains all around, I ran into another occupational hazard: sumptuous entertainment. In Attopeu it took the form of the Governor's noonday banquet of curry, accompanied by the rich, odoriferous fish sauce called *nam pa*. Pettenaro and the rest of the DC-3 crew dug in happily, while my stomach leapt, a light dew appeared on my brow, and I clung to the sides of my chair.

Back in Vientiane the doctor seemed singularly unimpressed. "Everybody gets things like that here," he said, and he never did tell me what he thought it was.

7 SAYABOURY AND THE ELEPHANT CHILD

SAYABOURY is a small province between Luangprabang and Vientiane, the only Lao territory on the right, or
west, side of the Mekong, and the center of the kingdom's
modest capture-training-and-export-of-elephants industry. It
was in Sayaboury that I was given a double baptism of Lao
weather and Lao entertainment.

The entertainment began at the airstrip, a little green hand-
kerchief with the knobbly mountains all around. Two pretty
little girls in traditional dress with buns at the backs of their
heads were there to present armfuls of flowers. My photograph was taken holding hands with somebody's pet gibbon.
I had come with Kampheng Vilay, a gentle, unworldly Lao
financier who lived next door to me at The Bungalow, and
Dr. Mary Slusser, an anthropologist who was doing a two-
year study of the peoples of Indochina for the State Department. Nivong and someone else from Prévoyance Sociale fol-

lowed us in another small plane, but they never got down; the fog spilled in over the surrounding mountains and did not lift for four days.

The only taxis in town were the Governor's jeep and the elephants, on which guests of honor were sometimes sent out to lurch around town, while the more susceptible ones tried not to get elephant sick. We took the jeep into town, down the main street of the provincial capital which looked like a lane in a Hollywood South Sea village. It was a happy, peaceful sort of place where the dogs were well kept and frisky, instead of the poor, hungry, cringing, three-legged, bony beasts one saw elsewhere in Southeast Asia. Bumping along, we tried to read the programs which had been handed to us, and which went something like this:

Arrival of Their Excellencies of the CARE	1600 Hours
Welcome by the Youth of Sayaboury	1603 Hours
Reception by H. E. the Governor at the Hôtel de Ville	1621 Hours
Address by H.E. the Governor	1625 Hours
Reply by Their Excellencies	1645 Hours
Traditional Ceremony of the *Bassi*	1700 Hours
State Ball	1730 Hours

and so on. I had no inclination to clock the Governor over the next four days, but my impression is that he produced everything as advertised, and managed to work in a few extra entertainments.

The gubernatorial mansion was another neat, cheerfully rustic house on stilts. We all said a few words on the porch, and then came the *bassi*, that uniquely Lao ceremony of welcome or farewell, marriage, greetings to a newborn child or a traveling dignitary, felicitations to a new mother or someone who has distinguished himself. As foreign visitors, we were it. We took off our shoes and socks, and knelt down in the Governor's parlor among a crowd whose hands were pressed together as they prayed for our health and good fortune. Before us on low round tables of woven bamboo and rattan were *repoussé* silver chalices holding offerings of plump little bananas, featherweight cakes made of exploded rice, betel leaves and areca nuts, an old beer bottle full of coconut milk, little bouquets of flowers tied with a small candle like those on a birthday cake, and some threadlike cords of cotton. The most venerable of the elders blessed us in a long singsong chant, invoking the divinities, while the young girls tied circlets of cotton around our wrists. The thirty-two souls who inhabit the body were asked to return home; as every Lao knows, they are notorious vagabonds, and there were special appeals to those who might have fallen into a hole, got lost in a river or a swamp or a pond full of frogs. When everyone felt confident that the divinities had arrived and all the souls had returned, we were congratulated.

An hour and a half later on the unroofed front porch we found ourselves in the middle of a *lamvong*, the national dance. I had hardly heard of the *lamvong*, and suddenly I found myself in the dismaying position of trying to lead one, with a tiny Egyptian-looking girl of nineteen beside me. She reminded me of the head of Queen Nefertiti, which was useful since it gave me something to think about besides my own helplessness. Except for New Year's Eve, I am barely able to get around a dance floor without tripping. I died a thousand deaths trying to figure out what to do next as we revolved in a large circle, two by two, with our hands tracing elaborately sinuous patterns in the air. At least all but one of us was.

The Governor of Sayaboury was a tall, thin, high-spirited type from the family who had built Vat Mixay in Vientiane. He had a flat nose, close-cropped hair with white sidewalls, and a head that went straight up and down in back; he was prancing along gracefully on the balls of his feet, just behind me. Behind him came the provincial veterinarian, a small golden-tawny man in a white drill suit, bending his fingers back as prescribed, until they looked double jointed.

The music went around and around like perpetual motion. There was one figure in which the dancers shot imaginary bows and arrows. In another, we played imaginary flutes and drums. There was a teasing number in which the partners turned to one another, and beckoned with one finger

come, come, come . . .
come, come, come . . .

only to hold up one hand like a traffic cop

STOP!

The music had a slight, synocopated hesitation. The orchestra was two two-stringed violins each played with a single stringed bow, a Lao xylophone, a drum like a giant tambourine, a lute, and a newfangled accordion, guitar, and banjo. The xylophone was called the *nang-nat*, a boat-shaped instrument played with mallets tipped with elephant's hide, and the violin, or *so-ô*, which was held nearly vertically, resting on the floor, had a very long neck and for a sound box half a coconut. There were falsetto whoops from the musicians, and the banjo player sang peppily, "Di-di-di-di-di."

In between each set of *lamvongs* we were entertained with Songs and Dances by the Schoolmistresses and Pupils of Sayaboury. It was hard to tell which was which, for they all looked sweet and modest and incredibly young. They were bashful but determined, and often as not they launched out with no accompaniment, chanting in a thin, quavery soprano, and ducking rhythmically. Six of them advanced and retreated, waving sprays of bougainvillaea. Then they waved long peacocks' tails, imitating the bird's courtship. I never knew that Laos had a Victorian period, but they sang songs with titles like "A Bent Blossom," "The Spouses like Turtle Doves," "Love in the Abyss," and "Mysteries of the Heart," to banjo accompaniment. At the end of each number the little master of ceremonies would say, "And now, the voice of the Schoolmistresses of Sayaboury is terminated" and "And now, the voice of the Sublieutenant is terminated. . . ."

"We are the most isolated and forgotten province in all of Laos," said the Governor aggrievedly. But the entertainment just wouldn't stop. There were four *lamvongs* in three days. It turned out that the schoolmistresses and their pupils not only were charming, but they could be charming all night, and if they ran out of songs, they just started all over again. I was dragged out to render an American song which the orchestra had just remembered, and when it turned out to be "Ach, Du Lieber Augustin," was obliged to recite it in French. Mary Slusser sang "Yankee Doodle." It was difficult to get any work done, and in the end, the ebullient Governor literally plucked me from my seat in front of a portable typewriter on the grounds that such behavior was wicked while the xylophone was playing and the maidens were doing the peacock dance.

The distribution of food packages had gone off well. Monsieur the Treasurer took it on himself to explain that the unfamiliar yellow cheese which was part of the package was nothing more than *paddek falang*, or foreigner's fish eggs. People laughed, and went home to try it.

It was good there was so much to do in Sayaboury, for it was cold, bitterly cold, damp and penetrating. In the morning, with the fawn and chalk colors of the Governor's bungalow melting into each other in the fog, we couldn't see across the narrow road. There was nothing there, just an aquarium full of cotton. Then, faintly, the outlines of the house across the way would become visible through the luminous mist, and by midday, if we were lucky, we could make out the head and trunk of Elephant Mountain groping in the clouds. The storm lanterns were lit inside the house. At night I went to bed wearing two pairs of socks, pajamas, Levis, a chambray shirt, a Canadian lumberjack shirt, and a Royal Navy surplus duffel coat. And I took a large glass of local brew called *shoum* before retiring. I was still cold.

The Governor's hospitality continued to be overpowering. It included cold fried eggs with sticky rice and *nam pa*, the essence of fish, for breakfast, together with venison leftovers and curried peacock. The mind boggled, or at least my mind boggled, when he called out briskly, "And don't forget to order an elephant for Madame le Docteur in the morning." Then he and his fellow dignitaries got out a box of marionettes, and made them jump around and wave through the window at the children leaning out of the house next door, until all the high officials were beside themselves with laughter.

We paid a visit to a nearby village where one of the celebrated Sayaboury elephants was being trained. This one was a rather annoyed little three-year-old, recently captured, but he was rapidly being soothed. In true Lao style, he was given plenty of sugar cane, and visited by bevies of young girls and their beaux who told him stories and sang songs, joked and chatted and danced about him so that he would become used to these social carryings on. Later, when he was more sophisticated, the young elephant would be taken for walks in the village, "so he will get to know life."

Bobbing around town on the back of a grown-up elephant in a contrivance that appeared to be a basket crossed with a prairie schooner, I learned that some of the Sayaboury alumni go to the royal elephant stables at Luangprabang, where every Lao New Year, at the Porch of Elephants, the priests whisper a special sermon in their ears. Some three or four Sayaboury-trained elephants are exported every year to Thailand, and once during a spat between the two neighbors, the Lao cut off the supply of elephants in an effort to bring the Thai to their senses.

Everything in Sayaboury seemed touched with gentle fantasy. One evening, returning to the Governor's at dusk, I saw a stubby witch capering in the twilight mist. It turned out to be a very small boy wearing his unicorn costume left over from the last great celebration.

8 THE LAND OF THE MILLION ELEPHANTS AND THE WHITE PARASOL

THE amiable-looking white elephant standing under his seven-tiered Buddhist parasol in a scarlet field now flaps bravely on the Lao flag at the United Nations. Of all the eighty-odd members, the elephant and his country are, by long odds, the least known.

As Lan Xan, the Land of the Million Elephants and the White Parasol, the little landlocked kingdom was a power on the peninsula. It still calls itself by its ancient name, and though the million elephants have been reduced to the modest exercise at Sayaboury and a few like it, a great deal of classical Laos survives in contemporary life. From Sayaboury to Saravane and back in Vientiane, I gradually absorbed a little of the history of the place.

The Lao Way of Life, which now seems fated to change abruptly, and perhaps somewhat awkwardly and uncomfortably, is the expression of an ancient, peaceful, Buddhist civil-

75

ization whose origins are lost in the mists of Chinese and Indian antiquity. All the Lao, so they say, are descended from the legendary Khoun Borom who came from the skies to south China, thoughtfully equipped with the regalia necessary for his own coronation, "mounted on a white elephant with beautiful black lips and eyelids, with curved transparent tusks which crossed, preceded by two women and followed by a long parade of horses, elephants, oxen, water buffaloes, scholars, mandarins, soldiers, pages and musicians, and six hundred matrons and maids of honor, advancing two by two. . . ."

This was the dawn of Lao time, part myth, part history, in that shadowy millennium between the third and fourteenth centuries A.D. when the Thai peoples were moving from Central Asia down through southern China and into the Indo-Chinese peninsula, driven before the Chinese and then the Mongols (the final straw was Kublai Khan who conquered the last Thai kingdom in south China in 1254). The Lao themselves are a branch of these Thai migrants. Thai and Thai-Lao people, speaking essentially the same language, are now spread across northern Vietnam, Laos, the Chinese province of Yunnan, northern Cambodia and Thailand, the Shan States of Burma, and all the way to Assam across the Indian frontier.

The Thai invaders conquered the Indonesian tribesmen settled around Luangprabang and Xiengkhouang and Vientiane, lumped them together inelegantly as *Kha,* or "Savages," and pushed them farther south. Khoun Borom's younger son, Khoun Lo, became King of Luangprabang, and some twenty-two kings followed him before the advent of Fa Ngoum, the father of the present kingdom and the ancestor of nearly all those who have reigned since his time. With him begins Lao recorded history.

It was Fa Ngoum who fled to Cambodia as a small boy, some six hundred years ago, when his grandfather, the King of Luangprabang, banished his father for conduct unbecoming to a prince. There, at the court of the Cambodian King Jayavarmaparameçvara at Angkor Vat, he studied with his Buddhist tutor. When he was about sixteen, Fa Ngoum was given Jayavarmaparameçvara's daughter, Princess Kêo, as his bride. A couple of years later he returned with an army lent him by the Cambodian monarch, conquering the little Lao kingdoms of Champassak in the south and Xiengkhouang in the north, and ultimately, in 1353, he subdued his grandfather at Luangprabang.

The country which Fa Ngoum united he called the Land of the Million Elephants. Thirty-two kings followed him until Laos divided, amoeba-like, in the early eighteenth century into the three kingdoms of Vientiane, Luangprabang, and Champassak. Many things happened. There were cultural invasions from Cambodia and from the vanished civilization of Champa in central Vietnam; there were military invasions from Burma and Thailand and China. In 1530 the sovereign issued an edict against the spirits known as *phis* (pronounced "p'hees"). In 1559, in the Lao-like words of one French historian, the reigning monarch "prudently refused combat" with the bellicose Burmese (matters were more peacefully arranged by making an alliance with the Thai).

Throughout all this, the Lao remained perfectly Lao. Sometimes the country was united under a single strong monarch, sometimes divided into separate petty kingdoms and principalities. But always a marked sense of cultural identity, Laoness, persisted throughout the whole area. The once fashionable Sanskritic names have faded: Vientiane, the Place of Sandalwood, is no longer called Candapurisisattanagamahanagara, nor Luangprabang called Sisattanaganahuta, the Place of Hundreds of Thousands of Cobras, but life goes on very much as when they were.

Gerrit van Wusthoff, the Dutch commercial traveler who was sent to Laos in the mid-seventeenth century by the Governor of the Netherlands West Indies to trade in stick-lac and benzoin, found the inhabitants amusing themselves with fireworks and entertained by maidens dancing with peacocks' tails. His Calvinist Dutch soul was repelled by the southern Lao town of Lakhon where he declared he was unable to take a stroll by moonlight because of the "horrible fornications" all around; but he found the procession of the twenty-three-year-old king with his elephants and horses and nobles and lancers and musketeers worthy of that of the army of the Prince of Orange. It was another hundred years before the Jesuit Father de Leria, somewhat indifferently received by the Buddhist bonzes, reported on the local scene, and another hundred years before the French explorer Pavie found himself following the same path, but they all reported in effect that the Lao were gentle, peaceful, innocent, charming, and a little feckless.

Three hundred years after van Wusthoff, the American economic missioners setting up camp beside the Mekong find stick-lac and benzoin still two of the country's major exports. The Lao are still Lao. They aren't really very angry with anybody, not even the French colonialists. Unlike the other Indochinese states, Laos is still a member of the French Union. Homer Bigart, then writing for the New York *Herald Tribune,* quoted the Lao Crown Prince, Savang Vatthana, as saying that in Laos no one ever suffered a nervous breakdown. Frustrated American sojourners retorted that if anyone did, it would be foreigners in the country administering economic aid.

Favorite Lao sports are still picnicking on Sunday, watching the sun set over the river Mekong, and playing badminton in the front yard. Storytelling is a major art. In Vientiane there are also a couple of movie houses showing Thai, Chinese, Japanese, Indian, and American films, and there is a spectacularly tumbledown house on the Street of Lost Joys which houses Thai and Lao theatrical companies; it advertises with a sound truck cruising around town blaring mysterious Oriental rhythms, occasionally with a small boy wearing a dragon suit jumping up and down in the back by the tailgate; some days there is a cavalcade of pedicabs, the first carrying a xylophonist, the second a base drummer, and the third a man with a signboard.

Buddhism came to Laos a couple of centuries earlier, but with the influence of Fa Ngoum and the priest and sculptors and scriptures they brought with them from Cambodia, it became the single greatest—and to the uninstructed foreign visitor, perhaps the happiest—influence in Lao life. Every self-respecting male in the kingdom, as in Cambodia and Thailand and Burma, is still expected, usually while quite young, to shave his head, wear saffron robes, and spend at least a few weeks of his life as a monk in a Buddhist temple.

The Lao have never lost their delight in festivals, sacred or profane. Usually they are a little of both. In the full moon of our month of May, which is the fifteenth day of the waxing moon of the sixth month of the Lao solar-lunar calendar, just before the rainy season, comes the Boun Bang-Fai, which is the triple celebration of the Birth, the Enlightenment, and the Death of Buddha. It is accompanied by religious rocketry, horseplay, and fertility rites. It is a combination street fair, ecclesiastical procession, fireworks display, carnival, picnic, tournament of chivalric balladry, and innocent bawdry of a kind that used to be nearly universal.

Bang-Fai means just what it sounds like. The rockets are twenty to thirty feet long, and the largest ones are charged with as many pounds of saltpeter. You can hear them whooshing and banging all over town. They are shot high over the Mekong to light the funeral pyre of the Buddha, but there is also an older explanation: Bang-Fai commemorates the wedding of a southern Lao princess when for three days rockets were launched skyward. The inhabitants of the heavens became fearful that the wedding guests were trying to set fire to them, and so appealed to the Hindu god Indra, who poured water over the fireworks. Hence, rain for the crops, brought on by firing rockets at the sky, and encouraged by a certain amount of ribald horsing around among the spectators.

The rockets are pious offerings to the Buddha. Each one is the loving creation of the fireworks master of some pagoda, or of eminent lay pyrotechnologists, and will defend the name of that pagoda and village before all comers. These days it may possibly represent some commercial corporation. The great rockets are propped up in a line above the crowd strolling along the riverbank, and the heads of the rockets look like Chinese dragons. It is the same with the beasts on the pagodas: they look much the same, but on the Chinese side of the cultural line that runs down Indochina, they are called dragons; on the Indian side, they are nagas.

Actually, they are supposed to be nagas, or cobras, survivors of an Indian snake cult now comfortably intermingled with Buddhism. It was a kindly naga who spread his hood over the Buddha to protect him from a flood, and the spirits who protected the old Land of the Million Elephants took the form of seven cobras who lived in a cave on the river above Luangprabang. At any rate, the skyrocket nagas are brightly painted, hung below with garlands and streamers and a multicolored pennant which symbolizes the rainbow, with a banner of crimson silk and the name of the hopeful pagoda stretched above, and a row of miniature parasols sheltering the naga's back, with perhaps a larger one over his head. The serpents' long bamboo bodies are decorated with geometrical designs pasted on in yellow, white, and green paper, red-and-gold, blue-and-silver, and some with little Lao national flags, with the three-headed elephant again, stuck in rows on their tails.

Fifteen gilded palanquins, shining with mosaics of gold and colored glass and topped with floppy ceremonial parasols and with nagas for armrests, head the religious procession led by the chief of the diocese of Vientiane. The skyrockets, their long tapering tails quivering elegantly, follow along behind. Women offer the bonzes gifts of flowers and little tapers of beeswax, slender sticks of incense, and jars of perfumed water. To the young men who have shaved their heads and are taking the monk's yellow robes that day, they bring the simple needs for a bonze's life: new cotton robe and sandals, begging bowl, fan, blankets and cushions, rice basket and water jug, knife and fork. The clergy retire to a pavilion in front of Vat Kang, overlooking the crowded street, and beyond, the bamboo scaffolding of the rocket-launching platforms, and the Mekong.

The crowd wanders back and forth along the riverbank or sits at tables set out in the grass, eating Chinese noodle soup or drinking the Siamese-American soft drink called Green Spot. There is a satisfied inspection of the skyrockets.

In a smaller open-air pavilion on the grass in front of the pagoda, there will be a musical duel. On the platform a musician kneels on one knee and plays an endless little melody on the *khèn*, a narrow panpipe of seven pairs of thin bamboo tubes with holes for fingering toward the center, just above a gourd mouthpiece surrounding the pipes. They run from a couple of feet to four or five feet long. The music is softly reedy, like a mouth organ but less harsh. While the *khèn* is playing, a man and a woman confront one another, singing alternately. The man asks of the woman what she knows of the birth of the Buddha, assuring her that if she cannot answer, she will be beaten. She knows a great deal, and sings verse after verse as the music jogs along. Then she calls on the man to tell her about the Buddha's life in heaven, or on earth. He replies at great length, and so it goes, while the crowd listens, fascinated.

A secular version of this has been going on since dusk of the evening before, with the gallants of Vientiane gathering one by one, or in small groups, with their friends accompanying them on the *khèn*, serenading the maidens of the town, extemporizing verses, paying flowery compliments, chaffing with their comrades, and vying with them for a glance or a song from the girl, who answers them in kind. These are the traditional Lao courts of love. And so, with faint echoes of medieval Europe, it goes on until the dawn. The young man politely asks in song after the health of the girl's parents, how the crops are going, what the food's like at home. The girl archly replies:

> The gnat lives as best it can
> On what nature provides.
> But how can a great white elephant
> Be interested in a little bamboo
> shoot like me?

This goes on for some time.

Meanwhile, bands of youths have been roaming from door to door, singing the traditionally improper songs expected at Bang-Fai, demanding from the mothers-in-law of the town tributes of alcohol or rice or salt fish. If refused, they are apt to make off with the ladder leading up to the thatched house on stilts.

The normally temperate Lao choose to drink only on festivals, but fortunately there are plenty of these. At the Bang-Fai they drink a sweet rice wine called *satho*, and by mid-afternoon the tipsier celebrants are dancing and weaving happily through the crowd, with improvised disguises that make them look like slightly larger children at Halloween, waving tattered parasols and wearing garlands of colored paper, beating on jerrycans and oil tins, waving and prancing, carrying furiously coupling male and female marionettes called *zobistes*, exhibiting homemade bawdy pictures to the crowd, and waving crudely painted wooden phalli at the ladies, who titter. All this helps the crops to grow.

At intervals a band of rocketeers will carry one of the gunpowder serpents, attenuated tail waving, on their shoulders to one of the launching platforms—high, rickety bamboo and rattan frameworks that look like skyscraper jungle-gyms, set up by the flame-of-the-forest trees overlooking the river. The whole business sways perilously as the launchers clamber about the bamboo grid, trying to set off the rockets. From time to time there is a tremendous whooosh. Some of the nagas arch high over the Mekong, bravely trying to reach the Thai west bank. The duds, which are numerous, whoosh backwards, spraying smoke and gunpowder over the crowd, and everybody laughs, and the launchers dance on the scaffolding. People make broad jokes about fertility in reverse.

Another explanation of the origin of all this carrying-on is that the festival celebrates the wooing of a beauty who was the daughter of the King of the Cobras and whose suitors were commanded by her father to launch rockets in competition for her hand. Now the competitor's entries bear such labels as the Mekong Waterways Transportation Society or the Vientiane Power Plant. In any case, the one that wins is bound to bring a year of success and happiness to the proprietor. The launchers of the losing rockets are taken up and down the street by the winners and offered to the local merchants cheap in return for a bottle of something to drink. Few merchants are tempted. The losers must buy. But this is Laos, and everybody has a glass together.

9 MORE ELEPHANTS, MORE PARASOLS

Laos and its people were mentioned from time to time in the chronicles of those indefatigable tourists the early Chinese and Indian travelers. But the outside world was barely conscious of Lan Xang and her neighbors in the thousand years that coincided roughly with the beginning of the Christian era, when the people who became Lao were moving down from southern China, and the Hindu and Buddhist cultures which found their way to this frontier of Further India slowly, gently changed until at last they became completely, inimitably Lao. Nobody even paid much attention in 1893 when France made Laos a protectorate, one of the several small kingdoms they pasted together in the administrative unit called Indochina.

Most of the outside, newspaper-reading world has heard of Laos only now after its invasion by the Vietminh and the long Communist administration of the two most northerly

Lao provinces which followed, the infusion of American aid until the Lao became, per capita, the most American-aided people in the world, the independence of Laos within the French Union, and the admission of Laos to the United Nations. Now the rest of the world has become faintly aware that there is a place called Laos, out there in the middle of the Mysterious East somewhere . . . a place in its own right. The outlanders who have turned up to administer foreign aid, to open diplomatic missions, to represent the UN, to serve on the International Control Commission are the latest in a long line of visitors—warlords, Buddhist missionaries, sculptors, opium traders, colonizers—many of whom have profoundly influenced the country.

Parts of the American way of life arrived with air conditioning when the American Legation was promoted to an Embassy, though the *chinoiserie* of dragons which ornamented the building was left undisturbed; with the American commissary which eventually appeared, to supply cigarettes and Campbell's soup, fruit juice and spirits, with the little tins of Nescafé that decorated every table, with the assortment of films borrowed from the U.S. military circuit in the region. Among the films was "A Yank in Indo-China," an acutely embarrassing hash of the Insidious Dr. Fu Manchu and Jack Armstrong, the All-American Boy, in which a squad of Mexican heavies and unemployed Japanese villains from Central Casting were put to work with Communist stars on their hats, playing the Vietminh. The Lao in the audience in the garden that night and those who were watching from the road didn't seem to mind, and laughed uproariously when anybody from either side bit the dust. Two-toned, fishtailed American cars have come to Laos to share the red roads with the oxcarts, the water buffaloes, and the barefoot market women with their baskets bobbing heavily from bamboo carrying poles. Somehow the cars contrive to look twice as long and vulgar overseas as they do at home. But things haven't yet reached the point in Laos that they have in Thailand across the river, where there are fishtailed pedicabs.

Sixty-one years as a French protectorate have left Laos with a French-speaking élite who run the country. Traditional French cultural patterns are preserved down to the official forms tinted a faded salmon or bluish dust color, and the dossiers secured with stringlike tapes, their covers lettered large in copperplate script out of an office pen. But the Anglo-Saxons have landed. When I arrived, in the Year of the Billy Goat, which was 1317 by Lao reckoning, 2498 on the Buddhist calendar, and a few days before the beginning of 1955 in the Gregorian, there were certainly not more than a dozen or so people in the kingdom with a working knowledge of English, including those in the Foreign Service. As this is written thirty-eight months later, in the Year of the Dog, there are probably several times that number, thanks to English lessons from the United States and the British Information Services, just a few doors from one another, an Australian English teacher provided by the Colombo Plan, and to the increasing number of Lao called upon to deal with the United Nations and the foreign missions, to work and to study abroad. Both Britain and America have been offering Lao scholarships in everything from animal husbandry to business administration.

Beneath these recent coats of varnish applied to the Lao pagoda by America and France and other emissaries from the outer world, all sparkling but rather thin so far, are the many layers of color left by the earlier Indonesian, Thai, Cambodian, Burmese, Indians, and Chinese. The migrations of

the Indonesian and Australasian peoples into Indochina a little before the dawn of Lao history, the early beliefs of the
Thai and their simple agricultural life have meant that an
unbudgeable animist belief in spirits called *phis* persists in
this otherwise devoutly Buddhist people, in spite of six hundred years' effort by the Buddhist clergy to disabuse them.
Among these *genii locii* are the spirits of the sky and the earth
and the crops, and the fifteen nagas who as water spirits live
in the rivers and their rapids and banks and grottoes and protect the kingdom. There are the spirits of the home and of the
family, who inhabit bright-colored shelters like birdhouses
sometimes found in the yards of even Frenchified houses in
Vientiane. Lumps of sticky rice are put out for these family
spirits, and in the dry season when the river is low, there are
little mounds at the edge of the sand flats stuck with joss sticks
and leaning reeds flying prayer flags, with flowers and bits
of sticky rice, offerings to the spirits of the water.

The *phis* to be avoided are those of wandering souls looking for something to eat (it is dangerous when traveling to
grill crabs or beef or fish, for the odor of their cooking attracts
the *phis*) or for a body in which to install themselves. There
are *Phi Pop* and *Phi Phong* and *Phi Kong Koi;* these last are
especially numerous in Samneua, one of the two ex-Com-
munist provinces.

There are many two-story buildings of brick and plaster in
Luangprabang and more in Vientiane that are as Gallicized as
those in any French provincial suburb. With varying degrees
of success, the Americans and other foreigners have rented
them. Americans have tried everything from the surplus US
Army tent which Carter de Paul first used as an office to the
gleaming aluminum prefab bungalows of the American compound. But the old legal decision of King Souligna Vongsa

in the mid-seventeenth century, about the time of the first European visitors, that the house of a Lao is one that stands on stilts and that of a Vietnamese (this could now be read as foreigner) is one that sits on the ground, still holds. Lao houses are handsomely suited to their climate and their surroundings. Everything is flexible, light and airy. An earthenware jug of water is cooling on a pillar near the house, there is a granary in back, and under the house there are a mortar for pounding rice and the narrow looms on which nearly every Lao woman is taught to weave. The Lao house is a bungalow in the traditional sense—a part of the common culture of South Asia where the monsoons bring the wet seasons and the dry.

The alternating seasonal winds of the monsoon carry the travelers across the Indian Ocean, through the Malay Archipelago, and around the Indochina peninsula into the South China Sea, filling the sails of all the dhows and junks from the Indian Ocean to the South China Sea. With India to the west and China to the east, the languages of Burma, Thailand, Cambodia, and Laos have inherited curly variations of the Sanskrit alphabet, while Vietnamese, until its romanization by Catholic missionaries, was written in Chinese characters. The Indian Ocean, the Gulf of Bengal, the Gulf of Siam, the Java Sea, and the South China Sea together form a sort of Mediterranean. The teachings of the Buddha that came to Laos in Sanskrit and Pali had spread from India through Ceylon and Indonesia, through the Malay and Indochina peninsulas, and on the north and east, as far as Tibet, China, Mongolia, and Japan. With the gentle doctrine of Buddhism and the religious texts came fables and exemplary tales, satires, sermons, wise saws, metaphysical treatises, epics and dance dramas, so that from Rangoon to Bangkok to Luangprabang to Angkor the dancers mime the endless variations of the story of Rama and Sita and the troublesome ogres and that valiant monkey general, Hanuman. Particularly popular in Laos are the 547 *Jâtakas* (twenty-seven of them known only in this country) which tell of the previous lives of the Buddha—king, student, wise man, courtesan, prince, Brahmin, actor, woodcutter, thief, slave, potter, mahout, or perhaps even a humble lizard or a buffalo, but always an example to all creatures in creation.

"Mother of wisdom, India brought her tales to her neighbors who were to teach them to the whole world," S. Lévi has written in his study *L'Inde Civilisatrice*. "Mother of faith and philosophy, she gave to the three-fourths of Asia a god, a religion, a doctrine, an art. She carried her sacred language, her literature, her institutions . . . to the limits of the known world." This was the fruit of Indian colonization. It was not imperialism, for there were no political ties to the mother country. The traders and the merchants and the settlers were brought by ocean-going junks, known for at least three centuries before Christ, ships which could carry six to seven hundred passengers. They sought the gold of an Eastern El Dorado and, more practically, the sandalwood, camphor, benzoin, the spices and the other luxuries so precious to Greece and Rome and the European hinterland, and so deplored by the Latin moralists of the first century.

With the merchants and the settlers came priests and architects. According to some admirers, Indian sculpture and the architecture of which it became an integral part found their greatest glory in the Cambodian temples around Angkor Vat and at Pagan in Burma. In Laos the decoration of the pagoda became almost as important as the pagoda itself, gracefully attenuated, essentially abstract in feeling, with flowers and beasts and demons and divinities carved and painted with an exuberance and a complexity that leaves no doubt as to the infinity of life and its perpetual transformation—dancing arms and legs and foliage and costume intertwined, fabulous beings whose tails and tongues end in convoluted flames.

In Laos live perhaps a thousand or so foreigners including some three hundred Americans, and a number of Indians, Poles, and Canadians with the International Control Commission. Most of the rest are French. There are also leopards and tigers and the small, not-very-pugnacious Siamese crocodile much sought after by naturalists, and a good supply of king cobras and kraits, and the few rhinoceroses who have escaped the agents of the relentless Chinese aphrodisiac dealers. There are several species of gecko, the bug-eyed, tender-skinned lizard which runs up the wall and across the ceiling, and chirrups in the night. People trying to describe the gecko's call have written it as *geck-o, check-o, tock-too, toc, toki, tokay,* and *chick-chick.* Among the other fauna of Laos are the water buffaloes, of course, the gaur, the pangolin, the peacock, the slow loris, and the common gymnure, or moon rat.

Flora includes teak, a little of which is exported. In the Lao villages the planting is the usual tropical mixture of bamboo, coconut palms, mangoes, banyans, figs, bananas, and bougainvillaea, morning glory, and hibiscus.

In the traditional Lao village economy there has been little need for trade, let alone imports and exports. Bamboo and palm are at hand to build light, airy houses, and the Lao grow enough glutinous rice, raise enough chickens, and catch enough fish in the rivers to get by except during occasional drought and famine as during the two years CARE worked in Laos.

Then, government revenues had quadrupled since 1950, but they still only came to about $17,000,000 dollars. Manufactures from abroad were imported in small quantities: $300,000 worth of cement for the whole country that year, and $400,000 worth of medicines, including Chinese herbal remedies; $1,750,000 worth of bicycles, pedicabs, jeeps, and other vehicles; $3,000,000 worth of gasoline; $2,500,000 worth of cigarettes and tobaccos, and about $1,000,000 worth of beer, *apéritifs*, champagne, still wines, spirits, and cordials, mostly French.

Laos still exports about three quarters of the fifty tons of benzoin used every year for perfume, stimulants, and expectorants, and a good many of the rest of the wares it sends to the world's market places are as special as Laos, and still read like the shopping lists of the classical Indian and Chinese traders. Laos exports annually 164 tons of the insect product known as stick-lac which is an ingredient in lacquers and varnishes; up to three thousand tons of green coffee; and, on the legal, medical market, roughly fifty tons of opium at about fifty dollars a pound. Opium finding its way into the illegal market is a major export, but there are, understandably, no statistics. Small quantities of cinnamon, cardamom, peanuts, cotton, quinine, rattan, chili peppers, pottery, dried mushrooms, hides, and areca nuts to chew with betel leaf are sold to neighboring countries. *Rauwolfia serpentina,* also known as snakeroot, was once in demand from Laos as a tranquilizer, but with the development of new synthetics the price has plummeted from twenty to five dollars a pound.

Since 1954, American aid to Laos has run from forty-three to fifty-three million dollars a year. Injected into a subsistence economy, this is enough to produce painful reactions, though so far serious inflation has been avoided. All but ten or twelve million dollars a year have gone to support the thirty-thousand-man Royal Lao Army which guards the traditionally tempting invasion route from China and North Vietnam into Thailand. As Buddhists, the Lao are reluctant to kill any living thing. But even the foreigners who despair that the Lao can be fired with enthusiasm for the techniques of the Western world do admit that they make first-rate parachute jumpers. During the dry season at Vientiane they can be seen at eight o'clock any morning floating down over the Mekong with little white puffs of parachutes, landing in the sand flats and laughing like schoolboys. They are light, well knit and with sturdy legs, docile in their acceptance of what this and future Buddhist lives may hold for them, and happy-go-lucky to the point where diving out into several hundred feet of thin air is a lark. One of the French jumpmasters who trained them, a man finely attuned to the Lao way of life, used to jump first to encourage his men, waggling his fingers in his ears and calling, "Cuckoo!"

About a quarter of America's economic aid has been going to make Laos' battered highways at least passable by jeep and truck and to provide some alternative to the pirogues and the antique steamboats on the shallow waterways, and the air transport which costs several times as much as in the United States or Europe. One of the last times I went through Vientiane, something like two million dollars worth' of phone-book-yellow earth-moving equipment was lined up in rows in the Cité Américaine compound, and trailers, jeeps, and bulldozers were to be added by the countries of the Colombo Plan.

The other three quarters of the money has been about equally divided between projects designed to encourage Lao agriculture, education, public health, and public administration. This is the job of USOM, the United States Operations Mission, which in Laos is the overseas arm of the ICA, or International Cooperation Administration, the alphabetical descendant of the Marshall Plan, ECA, MSA, Point IV, and FOA, and the sibling of STEM and TCM. (Personally, I am convinced that with Amtorg and Sovfoto and so on, the Russians are responsible for this dehydrated language.)

One of USOM's main jobs has been to restore some of the riches the country once had: a forestry program that will provide more lumber for woodworking, with reforestation at the same time so that the cutover areas in Laos don't come to look like the mountain wastelands of south China; conservation of benzoin and stick-lac; re-establishing the coffee and livestock trades, partly by improving strains of coffee and breeds of hogs and poultry; introducing once again simple systems of irrigation which in practice—and this sounds like a clumsy advertisement—literally double the rice crop.

Other foreign aid projects are beginning to take shape. UNESCO and some of the other United Nations specialized agencies have had a man or two in Laos, and the Colombo Plan countries have begun small but active programs. The Russian version of Point IV has at the moment still made no formal bid, but it is as close as Burma across the northwest frontier, and the Soviet delegate to ECAFE, the United Nations regional economic organization based in Bangkok, has made a general offer of assistance to all the Asian nations in sight. Chinese aid, already going great guns in Cambodia, and vociferously demanded by the Pathet Lao, is very possibly in the cards, too, but so far has been restricted to a couple of tons of gifts following the good-will visit to Peking of the incumbent Lao Prime Minister, Prince Souvanna Phouma.

Later, though I had by then left Laos, I happened to be on

my way through Vientiane, and was fortunate enough to have a chat with Prince Souvanna Phouma a few days after he had returned from a good-will mission to Peking. I had been in Hong Kong, and delayed a day because when I turned up at Kai Tak to take the Air Laos plane to Vientiane, I was told that it was being sent to Canton to pick up the Chinese government's presents to Laos and the Prime Minister. The next day, flying over the South China Sea, and giving a wide berth to Hainan Island where a Cathay Pacific airliner had been shot down a year or so before, I rode with the incense burners and the paintings and the twenty boxes of "ancient manuscripts concerning China and Laos" which the Peking government was supposed to have presented. Later, at the museum in Vat Phra Kéo, where the curators seemed to be wondering what to do with the opened cases, I had a chance to look at them, and they were a set of the beautifully reproduced Chinese classics published by the Commercial Press in Shanghai, first under the Nationalists, later under the Communists.

The Prime Minister had none of the presents with him in his office when I called, but he did have a dark wooden cigarette box mounted with a carved bird which picked up a State Express cigarette with its long beak and offered it to the visitor. He was delighted with the cigarette box. He is a strong but reserved man, gracious, beautifully mannered, solid, with heavy, peaked black brows, a shortish haircut, purplish lips, and rimless gold spectacles. He was in his shirt-sleeves, and wearing tan khaki trousers. He wore a conservative blue-and-gray-striped tie, a gold slave bracelet on one wrist, and a square gold ring.

Prince Souvanna spoke earnestly about the need for mineral exploration in Laos, potentially rich, as well as the modernization of the Thakek tin mines. He was right—there is uranium in Laos, though no one knew so at the time. He asked for artisans from Japan and India to teach in Laos. He felt that integration of the rebel Pathet Lao was just a matter of time —he was right about this, too—and looked forward to the time when money spent on the Lao army could be put into economic projects. The political winds seemed to be blowing Laos toward the nonalignment of Cambodia rather than the proclaimed anti-Communist, pro-American position of Thailand. "We would love to serve as an intermediary between the blocs," said Prince Souvanna Phouma as I left, "small country that we are."

I thought of the remark attributed to the Prince by a highly credible man who knows him well: "I am very proud of my connection with the Royal Family, and very proud of being a Prince. If the Communists come, I shall leave Laos. I shall never return."

The last word was had by my friend Pettenaro, the Air Laos navigator who had flown with the good-will mission to China.

Every day, people proudly said to the visitors, "Look, no flies. No flies at all." Finally, it became too much.

"Hah!" said Pettenaro. "They chose freedom."

French aid to Laos continues to be the most substantial after that from the United States, budgeted at about eight million dollars' worth of francs over a two-year period, and mainly used for rebuilding the roads linking Laos with Vietnam to the south; for the bright young men and women from metropolitan France who teach at the secondary and primary schools throughout the country; for the sixty or so Lao students who study in France; for radiological and surgical equipment in the hospitals at Vientiane and Luangprabang;

The Mekong flows peacefully through the Kingdom of Laos, and in the sacred grottoes in the bluffs above the River at Pak Ou, Buddhas upon Buddhas upon Buddhas line the caves.

Each Lao male is supposed to spend

at least part of his life as a monk,

or "bonze."

The Crown Prince leaves one of the grottoes. A few miles downstream before the steps of his palace the Royal Ballet performs the classic dance-drama, the Ramayana. Its fluid gestures and back-bent figures are echoed in the popular dance, the lamvong.

Dancing and drinking and cheerful bawdry at the Bang Fai festival before the monsoon: a crowd in the capital jokes about fertility, and country girls

come to town as

the bonzes shoot off rockets with

serpents' heads in an effort to pierce the

sky and make the rains come.

The rains come and the rice grows.
A man burns over a patch on the
mountainside and plants his crop. A
water wheel grinds the grain.

The work of women: under every Lao house the rice is hulled with a giant mortar and pestle whose beam is operated by foot. Silk is spun, and sarongs and scarfs and tropical tartans are woven.

The work of men: the Lao carpenter is armed with a coupe-coupe and a bamboo scabbard. Beside the Mekong a man weaves a part of his house. An elephant helps build it.

But all is not work, and the Lao insouciance is catching: a pet gibbon swings from an American flagpole; a small boy carrying spaghetti tucks flowers in his turban; pedicab drivers at the market doze in the noonday shade; a whimsical naga rears skyward from the corner of a pagoda; and a wall supports two revelers, one of them playing a mandolin.

The eternal Laos: mountains and mist,

swooping rooftops and houses on stilts,

children, parasols, and jungle fowl.

and for creating an airport at the old flying buffalo corral at Vat Tay in Vientiane. Japan and the United States have been working jointly on a project to send Japanese specialists in animal husbandry, coffee and rice culture to Laos, together with some young Japanese to settle on the land as farmers, as is being done in Cambodia. Thailand has contributed five hundred tons of rice, and antimalarial teams to help stamp out the disease in Laos as has very nearly been done in Thailand; Australia has sent relief shipments of potatoes, and radios for village notables to get the news from Radio Vientiane where the voices of French and Lao disk jockeys are flung into the Indochinese ether from a transmission tower provided by US aid. India can be expected to offer agricultural and cultural talent, just as she has sent a professor of Sanskrit to Phnom-Penh. After CARE's arrival, International Voluntary Service turned up to run a notably successful agricultural extension service around Xiengkhouang, and the Philippine Junior Chamber of Commerce's remarkable medical effort called Operation Brotherhood turned up. Laos is wide open. One can only hope that more international, national, and private groups can find the way.

Among the most promising of all the foreign aid projects in Laos so far seem to be those to foster stock raising, poultry and rice growing; to teach sanitation and hygiene, make simple medical kits available in the villages, and eliminate both malaria and yaws; and to make full use of the new railway from Bangkok all the way to Nong Khai across the river from Vientiane, which has finally given the Lao reasonably convenient access to the sea, and should bring down the fantastic cost of living in the Lao capital. The malaria campaign alone is of tremendous importance. Probably the greatest killer the world has ever known, and certainly the heaviest brake on human productivity and the cause of as much plain misery as anything ever known, malaria has only been conquered since the development of the insecticides and prophylactics of the past few years. At the same time, public health people have discovered that malarial mosquitoes become hardened, after a bit, to DDT and the rest, so if malaria is to be successfully stamped out, it must be attacked at once, and on at least a national, or preferably regional, basis. In an area like northwest Laos, with people, and mosquitoes, happily crossing over the frontiers of Laos, Thailand, Burma, and China, all with different programs, politics, resources, and attitudes, this poses a problem. But somehow, people are going to have to learn to co-operate. An ironical little warning of what can happen if we don't was given by the Asian flu epidemic of 1957. Discovered in north China, the virus was isolated in Peking fully two months before it turned up in Hong Kong, and was finally reported from Singapore to the World Health Organization.

A similar problem is inherent in the Mekong River survey being conducted for the United Nations by the US Army Engineers' retired Lt. Gen. Raymond Wheeler. The present survey, following a preliminary one by USOM out of Bangkok, is in many ways one of the most exciting of all the plans to change the Southeast Asian future. Undertaken at the request of Laos, Thailand, Cambodia, and South Vietnam, the survey is likely to lead to multipurpose dams providing irrigation, electricity, flood control, and navigation along the lower course of a river that is just a little longer than the Mississippi. Willard R. Espey, whose magazine articles recommending that technical and economic aid be given to other areas of the world were one of the sparks which kindled President Truman's Point IV, has now recommended that

the Mekong River project be an international collaboration
between American and Russian engineers. This proposal has
interesting ramifications, for the Mekong River begins its life
flowing through Tibet and China.

The young Lao government which must struggle with these
problems is a constitutional monarchy, with an elected National Assembly of thirty-nine deputies and a Royal Council,
two-thirds appointed by the King, which acts as a sort of
Upper House and can veto legislation unless repassed by a
two-thirds majority in the Assembly. There are eleven members of the Cabinet, one of whom leads the government as
Prime Minister and Secretary of State for Interior, a post
which has alternated in recent years between Katay Don
Sasorith and Prince Souvanna Phouma. Two recent Cabinet
Ministers were members of the old Pathet Lao rebel hold-
outs, oddly enough responsible for religion and for the foreign aid programs, including the American. Four major parties
and 228 candidates for deputy contested one of the first national elections, largely on a personal basis, covering their
constituencies by paddle pirogue and motor pirogue, truck
and jeep, pony and light plane. It is true that Laos is still a
semifeudal country, largely governed by a few great families,
but the 228 aspirants caught on quickly, dandling babies and
handing out aspirin, showing movies, throwing parties with
free drinks and dancing, and putting their pictures up everywhere, including the backs of pedicabs. Representative government has arrived.

10 STILL LAN XAN

THE country which the thirty-nine legislators and their Cabinet of eleven must administer is an elongated amoebalike blob which covers some ninety-one thousand square miles, but beyond that, most statistics are guesswork. Not only has Laos no railroads, but there are not more than a dozen or so high school graduates a year. There are no chemists or agronomists, few engineers and no lawyers, though there are judges, and deputies to the National Assembly may plead before the courts. There is one general.

But there are strange stirrings in the drowsy Lao air these days, and each Tuesday and Friday morning the American government courier plane that flies between Saigon, Phnom-Penh, Bangkok, and Vientiane dumps a new cargo of electric generators, agricultural experts, malaria-fighting equipment, and other tools of American aid at the airfield at Vat Tay. There have been reconnoitering parties of Thai, British, Japa-

nese, Swiss, Chinese, Danish, Indian, and Pakistani business-
men, all scenting new money in the air. The ferment is beginning to affect even the gently moving Lao who have been
rushing off to international conferences on Buddhism, Afro-
Asian affairs, public health, SEATO, the Colombo Plan,
telecommunications, meterology, fishing, housing, statistics,
waterways, forestry, crime prevention, rice selection, atomic
energy, railways, and large dams. Laos has turned up at ex-
positions in Seattle, the Dominican Republic, and Cambodia.
And with a dispatch that would command respect on our own
Capitol Hill, a couple of dozen of the parliamentarians in the
new Lao legislature have sent themselves on *voyages d'information* to Japan, Burma, France, and the United States. Laos
has been recognized by half a hundred governments, including those of Spain, Norway, Liberia, Luxembourg, and the
Holy See.

The climate of Laos is, as they say, monsoonal, steamy in
the summer in the lowlands and chilly in the mountains and
high plateaus, with a relatively dry winter and spring and
heavy rains the rest of the year that leave a good deal of the
country unapproachable except by dugout or by helicopter.
But there are no helicopters except a couple of French Army
ones used by the International Commission. Doors bang vio-
lently in the wind when the monsoon comes, the rains beat
against the thatch and tin roofs, and the curly pods of the
flamboyant trees explode with a sharp crack like gunfire. The
cicadas, in the heat of the day keening like a distant sawmill,
at night come banging into the light. Yet even with the deluge
the water supply keeps giving out, and the tank truck which
makes the rounds of Vientiane fails to arrive. And the handsome, metallic green-black and golden-russet local cock,
scratching about the houses on stilts is undeniably *Gallus*

gallus gallus, the classical Burmese jungle fowl who is the ancestor of all our barnyard chickens. Except that in Laos the bird has succumbed to the national *dolce far niente,* and instead of crying Cock-a-doodle-doo! or the brave French *Ko-ko-ri-ko!'* the Laotian rooster goes *Euk-leu-u-u-u,"* giving a remarkable imitation of a gramophone running down.

The great tropical trees on the bank are festooned with epiphytes and creepers. The band of exuberant foliage on the far bank is Thailand. An occasional pirogue, dark and slender, with high, curly snouts at bow and stern, floats diagonally across the surface of the water. At the river's bend, just upstream from Vientiane, are long, low lines of mountains, lavender and blue-gray, cloud hung, and shining in the late afternoons. At sunset the clouds and the sampans are reflected in the water, and women are washing themselves and their sarongs, their hair glistening blue-black, and their children frolicking around them like brown minnows. There is the dull, low booming of a drum calling the monks to prayer, and down the road that winds along the river wanders a man in a tattered shirt and a black-and-white-checked sarong that looks like an old tablecloth, lost in the plaintive air he plays on his *khèn.* Quietness and peace are in the air. It seems unthinkable and monstrous that these people are in danger of being turned into pastoral robots by their dedicated neighbors.

The Lao's explanation of their origin is straightforward: an envoy of the King of Heaven took a red-hot iron and thrust it into a large pumpkin, whereupon all the Khas, the aborigines in these parts, tumbled out, a little darkened by the ashes; they were closely followed by the lighter-skinned Lao.

According to the most conservative estimate of the anthropologists of the École Française d'Extrême-Orient, something less than half of the population of Laos is made up of Lao, that is, the original Tibeto-Burman stock, the rest being Ho, Kho, Meo, Yao, Musso, Kha, Black Thai, White Thai, Lu, P'hunoi, and a welter of other ethnic minorities, all scrambled until a colored ethnographic map of Laos looks like a Cape Cod spatter floor. The province of Haut-Mékong in the northwest is in fact nothing but minorities, about twenty-eight of them, and a handful of Lao civil servants running the show.

Most of these tribespeople are mountaineers, poorer than the Laotian Laotians, and with even fewer schools and dispensaries, the last in line for government jobs (about the only jobs there are so far), and until recently, largely ignored by the dominant Lao minority.

Some of the minorities have acquired a new importance in these politically tricky times. Thailand as a member of the Axis was enthusiastic about enrolling under her own banner all the Thai peoples including those in Laos, Cambodia, south China, and North Vietnam. After the war the Vietminh supported a loose, semiautonymous Thai confederation in North Vietnam, and after the Communists came to power in China, they invented their bogus Free Thai Autonymous Republic in Yunnan. A Pan-Meo or Pan-Thai movement is always a latent possibility among the people who spread across the same frontiers, and there have been some inroads by Communist agents among the Moi in Central Vietnam and the Kha in Laos. Persuasion has taken every form from impressing unsophisticated tribesmen that the strange visitors who come to live among them are really magicians and can turn themselves into tigers at night unless the tribesmen all join the correct political party, to covering the village circuit with ballad singers with a message. It is difficult to judge the success of such efforts, but it is thought the Communists have made some progress. In a rural way, it is oddly reminiscent of the more citified efforts of the Communist party to capture the American folksong movement during the thirties and forties: during the Second World War a good many parties in Greenwich Village ceased to be just parties when the innocent New Yorker, looking forward to a pleasant evening with friends of friends whose gathering was to be enlivened by one of the better ballad singers, suddenly found himself asked for 29 cents at the door, and 34 cents for each drink except scotch, which was 43 cents. When there was a lull somebody asked him to sign a petition supporting the Soviet demand for a Second Front.

In Laos, half a world away, at the bottom of the heap are the Kha, a loose local term for a number of tribes of Indonesian stock who were the early inhabitants of the region, perhaps preceded by Astraloids, Melanesoids, and the Asian Pygmies called Negrites. The Khas tend to be a burnt-toast color, a bit darker than the average Lao, as explained in the legend of their liberation from the pumpkin. They wear long hair and a little fore-and-aft *cache-sexe* which doesn't hide very much, and they smoke short, fat conical cigarettes. They are fond of planes, and used to love to inspect our Air Laos craft after we had finished unloading packages. The southern Lao mountains where the Kha live can be miserable. The Kha have inadequate campfires and no blankets, and they suffer bitterly from cold and pulmonary trouble. They are shy, but curious. At one time the Kha became so annoyed at being treated like second-class citizens by their Lao masters that, in the neighborhood of Saravane, the Royal Army was reluctant to send out patrols because the Kha had taken to digging pits in the trails and covering them with branches and leaves.

Like the Kha, many of the Meo are animist, shamanist, or even Christian, rather than Buddhist. There have been a few American Protestant missionaries in Laos for about thirty years now, but the Lao show a marked inclination to remain Buddhist; it is largely among the spirit-worshiping tribes-people that the missionaries have been successful. Between the sixteenth and the mid-nineteenth centuries, the Meo filtered down from China, and in Laos they now live in iso-lated villages on mountain tops throughout the country. They like to wear dark blue with touches of scarlet, black silk mandarin beanies, and great, rounded dog collars made of silver. Some of the Meo women wear their hair twisted in an enormous, doughnut-shaped roll of horsehair, and though they live in the cool mountain country, they like to work naked to the waist. Nearly all of the Meo raise opium. In their white poppy fields in the dark green northern moun-tains, they produce most of the first-class opium for which this region is famous. Two crops a year move from Burma, Yunnan, north Thailand, Laos, and North Vietnam, down through the Bamboo Curtain if necessary, and on to Bang-kok, Saigon, and Singapore, through Hong Kong, and then out to Europe and the United States. At the same time, a cheaper grade of opium from the Middle East moves up through Malaya and Indochina into China for the market there, in spite of the strict prohibition of the Communist authorities. Many well-informed people in the region have scouted the contention of the US Treasury's Bureau of Nar-cotics that the Chinese Communist government is officially encouraging the export of drugs in order to earn foreign ex-change, and to undermine the enemy, but at least the first part of this does seem possible according to a scholar of my ac-quaintance who visited the opium-growing region of Yunnan, and is convinced that the open cultivation and export there would be impossible without the approval of the government.

Whatever the ramifications of the international drug traffic —and in spite of the fears of the narcotics experts at the United Nations and elsewhere that the greatest danger in the future, in this increasingly addicted world, lies in the production of synthetic drugs rather than the production of opium and its derivatives—still the fantastic profit to be made by the successful smuggler of narcotics makes the business next to uncontrollable.

Another problem, now being faced in Iran by the UN and the Iranian government and one which will have to be faced one day in Laos, is how to provide an adequate alternative crop to the farmers who now raise opium. No one has yet found the answer.

The French colonial government allegedly took care of some two thirds of the cost of running the Lao protectorate with profits from the government opium monopoly. Whatever the profits, they are now going into private hands. The fifty to one hundred thousand Meo who raise the stuff are sturdy, well armed, and, so far, fairly independent politically, largely in control of the territory which they inhabit. It's hard to tell how many there are, for, as in some other lands, inhabitants upcountry are notably reluctant to admit they exist lest they be taxed or conscripted.

Among many of the remote non-Lao villagers, a sense of Lao nationality is hazy or nonexistent. There are numbers of people in the country who have never heard of Vientiane or Luangprabang, or of their King, Sisavang Vong, or even of the Kingdom of Laos. One of the primary jobs of the Royal Lao Government is to make the Kha and the Meo and all the rest aware of themselves as a part of the nation. A good deal of the material put out by the local USIS attempts to do just this—a colored portrait of His Majesty Sisavang Vong for each village classroom has been a big hit, and, discretely, there is no mention of the United States. The idea, sensibly, is that if people are to defend their country, they must first be aware of what it is they are defending. American propaganda in Laos hasn't fallen into the trap that it did next door in Thailand, where for a time until it was abandoned, there was an intensive program to explain to the simplest country people exactly where international Communism was wrong. On the grounds that then one had to go to the trouble to teach people what Communism is, USIS in Laos simply referred to the Vietminh forces as foreigners and invaders. The Pathet Lao, on the other hand, fell more and more into the classical propaganda pattern, and in their broadcasts over Big Brother's Radio Hanoi were blaming all the world's woes on the United States, and denouncing the Royal Government for accepting American aid while the peaceful Lao skies were filled with parachuting Yankee spies. In the two northern provinces of Samneua and Phongsaly, and on occasion down into Luangprabang province and other areas adjacent to the Communist-held territory, mobile Vietminh teams were making friends and influencing people with propaganda films, one of the most effective of which was a documentary made at Dienbienphu where fellow Asians beat the foreign white imperialists. There is little antiforeign feeling in Laos, but the spectacle of the fighting could be frightening to the villagers who watched the pictures.

It was first the Japanese, then the Pathet Lao who broke the long Lao siesta. The dream of peace was shattered. The Pathet Lao began as a resistance movement dedicated to wresting home rule from the French who moved back in 1946 after the brief Japanese occupation of the kingdom. The Pathet Lao Issara, or Free Laos, movement operated in exile from Bangkok, and included most of the figures in the present Royal Lao Government, in particular Katay Don Sasorith and Souvanna Phouma. In Bankok they formed a shadow Lao government and carried on a propaganda war against the French and against the Lao Crown Prince, Savang Vatthana, for cooperating with the French. Mr. Katay, a short bustling man whose name in Lao means "rabbit," wrote tracts by the dozen, signing himself "Don Sasorith," "Arsène Lapin," and "William Rabbit." After three years, when the French offered semi-independent status within the French Union, most of the group packed up and came home, except for the shadow government's chief, Prince Petsarath, who held out for his old title, Viceroy of Luangprabang (he finally got it, and came home at last), and a minority of extreme nationalists who continued to call themselves Pathet Lao, and who in the end accepted the help of the Vietminh. Just to confuse matters, the name Pathet Lao, which they succeeded in getting the outside world to call them, means "Lao Nation" and is the Lao's own name for their country—rather as though a group of successful Communists were in control of most of Vermont and New Hampshire, which they then persuaded foreign countries to call "America."

Those who wanted to make Laos over into a country cousin of China and North Vietnam had a good toehold in the northern provinces of Samneua and Phongsaly, just across the Communist frontiers, which made supply as easy as it was likely to be in back-country Laos. There, in the magnificent green mountains thinly settled by the northern tribes, malarial, lost in mists during the rainy season, then hidden in the *brume sèche* of the ricefields being burned for planting, the rebel

Pathet Lao set up rustic Communist capitals in the two provincial centers, also called Samneua and Phongsaly. These village strongholds were complete with disciplined youth movements, rice requisitioning, propaganda theater, and manifestations in favor of peace. It was in these two areas that the Pathet Lao were supposed to "regroup" their forces according to the terms of the Geneva Agreement, withdrawing from all other parts of Laos. They regrouped all right, and the foreign troops apparently went home (until this point, most of the patriots liberating Laos turned out to be Vietnamese or Chinese). But instead of keeping their army to the two thousand stipulated at Geneva, the Pathet Lao increased it to somewhere over five thousand. Arms were supplied from across the border, and in great part the Pathet Lao's new weapons were American, captured by the Communists in China or supplied by the United States to the Vietminh guerillas during the war against Japan.

A further complication not untypical of Asia these days was that many of the leaders of the invading Pathet Lao forces and of the Royal Lao Government were old schoolmates, colleagues, or close relatives. Just as the members of the Vietminh and South Vietnam governments grew up together and worked on both sides, as the ex-Emperor Bao Dai served under Ho Chi Minh, and as two of the famous Soong sisters, Madame Chiang Kai-shek and Madame Sun Yat-sen, are persons of greatest consequence in Nationalist China and Communist China, respectively, so Prince Souphannavong, the leader of the Pathet Lao, is a half brother of Prince Souvanna Phouma, the Lao Prime Minister. All through the fighting between the two sides, and in the face of considerable skepticism from foreign observers, the feeling persisted among Lao that Pathet and non-Pathet were all Lao together, and between themselves they could sort out their differences if the Vietminh would just leave them alone. This turned out to be true. It is fair to say that the Pathet Lao was a puppet government. The Vietminh supplied political and military direction as well as the original manpower. One can imagine the Vietminh's experts-on-loan, like their opposite numbers in the American foreign aid programs to the south, muttering about the impossibility of getting anything done in Laos. Certainly the ineffable Lao seem unlikely material for rural Marxists, or Uncle Ho's "Disciplined Joy," but then, so must have seemed many of the tribal peoples of the Soviet Union and China, including the Lao's own cousins in Yunnan. The Pathet pupils had some five years of politico-military indoctrination. It remains to be seen whether the vaccination took.

The skirmishing that went on in Laos was never decisive. Both sides seemed to be holding back a little. All through the trouble, the Pathet Lao insisted they acknowledged the sovereignty of King Sisavang Vong. They just kept shooting up his troops, and took over all airstrips in Samneua big enough for even the smallest light plane. I went one day to call on the then Royal Governor of Samneua who had been forced to abandon his provisional provincial capital under attack, was lucky enough to escape in disguise, and was now down with malaria in the small shop which he kept in Vientiane. He showed me a telegram he had received that day from an officer in one of the posts in Samneua still held by the Royal Army. It read in French: PLEASE PARACHUTE MY PAY.

The International Control Commission, with Polish and Canadian members and an Indian chairman, was charged in each of the three Indochinese states with inspection on both sides of the line to make sure that the terms of the cease-fire were being carried out, and to work toward a political settlement in each country. The difficulty was the old familiar obstacle in Korea: the Commission had no power of enforcement, and even its theoretical right of free observation could be blocked in a thousand ways by the authorities on either side. There were charges of breeches of the agreement on both sides in all three countries, of course, but the most consistent and credible charge has been that in North Vietnam, as in North Korea, there was an immediate, heavy military build-up in contravention of the Geneva Agreement, which the Communist authorities had agreed to abide by.

Vietnam was divided at the 17th parallel, as Korea had been at the thirty-eighth. Matters were eventually patched up in Cambodia where there had also been a small-scale Vietminh invasion. Laos was left teetering. But the Pathet Lao operated against a disadvantage: whereas in Vietnam the Communists took over a nationalist struggle against French colonial authority, the invasion of Laos was aimed at the Lao's own government, itself trying to wrest home rule from the French. Jawaharlal Nehru had made it clear on his visit to Ho Chi Minh in Hanoi in 1954 that India considered the independence of Cambodia and Laos (on the Indian side of Indochina) to be of first importance, and some thoughtful foreign observers consider that this more than any other single factor may have drawn the line that has kept Cambodia and Laos free enough to work out their own destinies. In any case, the situation in Laos was fluid, though the word is hardly strong enough to describe it. Fluid and unpredictable. And Lao. There was just a chance that the International Commission, which during my sojourn was led by a witty, patient, and extremely capable man named Samarendranath Sen who had been Indian Consul General in Geneva, would work out an accommodation.

So Vientiane was full of Polish officers, Canadian officers, and Indian officers. In the smoky blue haze of the early morning a long line of white jeeps rolled down the arcades of tropical trees in Vientiane, collecting the members of the ICC. They brought a further cosmopolitan flavor to a town that was already remarkably international. A village of Black Thai refugees from around Dienbienphu was establishing itself down the road, and Pakistani merchants were moving in. It was not remarkable, perhaps, that an American chargé d'affaires should have been posted to Vientiane from Kabul, which he reached overland from Moscow, but it was a little surprising to find two dozen people in town fluent in Spanish, and a French girl named Peggy Martin, working for USIS, who was essentially a Hebrew scholar. Among the French Negro troops known collectively as Tiralleurs Sénégalais I ran into individuals from French Guiana, Martinique, Guadeloupe, the Ivory Coast, and the Congo, many of them homesick for Paris and Marseille.

There was also something slightly unexpected about the mixture of Polish and Indian foods in the ICC mess: a formidable mixture of vegetable curries, jars of pickled hot peppers, Polish peasant soups, dhal and rice, cabbage and sausages, and deep-fried breaded pork.

Four times a week the DC-3 of the International Commission touched down at Vientiane on its way to Phnom-Penh and Saigon or to Uncle Ho Chi Minh's Hanoi. Vientiane is at the end of the long Polish courier run from Russia across Russia and China and through North Vietnam. It is roughly at the antipodes from New York. It was a novelty to see one of the Polish films, with the credit "Script Girl" in pure American, and the "newsreels" of happy folk dancing, but in the end the program was even more dismal than some of the

Hollywood exports. Much more interesting were the reporters and the stray visitors who were dropped by the courier planes. The first year I knew Laos, there were exactly two American tourists, a young couple who arrived in spite of all dire warnings and the ineffectual efforts of American diplomats along their way to discourage them. To American officials familiar with the board and lodging available in Vientiane, the thought of an American tourist was traumatic. One bona fide British tourist did arrive, a very friendly man named Simon Read who spoke Cantonese, and carried a large pair of binoculars with which he immediately lit out for the bush; he explained that he was bird watching, but almost no one in Laos had ever seen a bird watcher, so sophisticates decided he must be a spy. It was Mr. Read who told me about *Gallus gallus gallus.*

11 *BOUNS* AND PAGODAS

THERE was little organized, or even disorganized, entertainment when I came to live in Vientiane. There was an occasional soccer match between two of the provincial centers down at the small stadium. Just across a mud rut from the stadium was an open-air night club called the Pam-Pam operated by a young viscount and two other youthful adventurers from Paris, the forerunner of a number of honky-tonks on the Lao Klondike. There were no bookshops, though I could get orders from Foyle's in London in a couple of months or so, with luck, and every once in a while I exchanged batches of the International Edition the New York *Times* with Wells Klein and Jacques Lauriac for the Paris *Trib*.

For any true Lao in need of good cheer and companionship the thing to do is not to hang around the post office, but to go to a *boun*. *Bouns* are easily the most popular amusement in Laos. And they are certainly the most Lao. The word in

Sanskrit means to give alms, to gain merit, and the essential, religious heart of a *boun* is always prayer. There are offerings of flowers and food, candles and incense before images of the Buddha. There are special prayers and sermons, and alms for the bonzes.

The pagodas are filled with bright paper flowers like party favors—white and lemon, pink and crimson clusters in the dusk—beeswax candles and smoking joss sticks, and softly gleaming golden images of the Buddha. The pagodas are schools and community centers as well as places of worship and the source of Lao art and architecture, music and dancing, and most of the rest of Lao culture. The monks belong to the Mahanikay and Thammayat orders of the Theravada or Southern School of Buddhism practiced in Laos, Thailand, Cambodia, Burma, and Ceylon. In colonial French the monks are called bonzes, and the small boy novices are called bonzillons, and they all live together in a bonzerie. The bonzes and the bonzillons are studying English now as well as French and the sacred texts on corded strips of palm leaf, and in the monastery courtyards they watch showings of some of the hundred or so films from the USIS film library: "Bryn Mawr," "A Boat Excursion on the Hudson," "Junior Chamber of Commerce," "The Human Body," "Tuberculosis," "Toscanini," and "Vice-President Nixon."

At any *boun*, everyone walks slowly, clockwise, three times around the pagoda before midnight. Different *bouns* celebrate holy days and holidays: one commemorates the meeting, just before his death, of the Buddha with the demon Mara, when the Buddha said, "Do not be upset, Sly One; in three months I shall be in Nirvana." Another honors the Buddha's incarnation-before-last, when, as Prince Vessantara, he was exiled by his people who were annoyed because he had given away his kingdom's white elephant. The elephant could bring rain whenever it wanted to. Then the prince gave away as alms in his wanderings his chariot, his horse, his children, and his wife, in that order, before all ended happily. There is Vientiane's famous fireworks fête with the naga rockets. And above all there is the Lao New Year (which naturally comes a little late, during the sixth month in the Lao calendar), when there is a parade of the royal elephants, everyone douses everyone else in sight with colored water, birds and beasts are bought from vendors especially to be set free, and live fish are charged with all of the faults of the past year and then put back into the Mekong to swim away with them.

If the Lao are deeply Buddhist, they are also relaxed and fond of jollifications. What with the loud-speakers grinding out Thai and Lao dance music, you can hear a *boun* long before you can see one.

To have a *boun* has come to mean simply to have a festival, a public party, to raise money for the pagoda. To raise money for the pagodas, the members of each one give at least one *boun* a year, and frequently more, turning the grounds around the temple into a pleasure garden. Since there are some eighty pagodas in Vientiane, and each *boun* lasts several days, there is generally a good choice during the nine months' dry season, until the Buddhist Lent begins with the rains, and the bonzes are restricted to the pagodas lest they take the life of the least living thing walking abroad during this creeping, crawling season.

At the entrance of a *boun,* past the tangle of onlookers, pedicabs, and Chinese soup wagons, and under the strings of colored lights and paper flowers will be a cluster of young girls who worship at the pagoda. They are like butterflies in the flickering light, the gold embroidered borders shining on their best silk scarves and skirts as they offer the visitors small candles tied in miniature, old-fashioned bouquets wrapped in cones of green leaf. Inside the pagoda grounds, in rows along the sides of the temple, are rows of market women, usually the prettiest young girls of the surrounding villages come to town to make friends or catch a husband, sitting on handsome stools about five inches off the ground and before round tables not much higher, all made of rattan and split bamboo, and if you ever bought some to take home, termites. The girls' faces are softly lighted by the tiny kerosene lamps on their tables, and they sell hardboiled eggs and chicken wings, plastic toiletries and cheap Indochinese French cigarettes that somehow turn out to be made by the British and American Tobacco Company, slices of cucumber, balls of sweetened popped rice, and small glasses of *shoum,* the national drink, distilled from rice or corn or both, faintly frosted, slightly sweet, and not bad at all.

At the *boun* there are weight-guessing and fortunetelling booths presided over by the boy bonzillons, Chinese gambling games, and Thai foot-boxing, a little like the French *savate,* but with an orchestra of flutes, cymbals, and drums that accompanies the falls with crashes and tootles. Often there is an open-air screening of USIS films, and sometimes a Thai-Lao provincial theatrical company which brings the house down with low-comedy pratfalls and pop songs screeched into the microphone. Amplifiers are known in Laotian as "big mouths," but they seem to be popular, something I don't quite understand in so gentle a people.

The atmosphere at a *boun* is a cheerful blend of a church supper and a country fair. It is much the same at a Lao funeral, and these can go on for three days. However, the *bouns* are public, and everybody goes: French and Lao soldiers together, Poles and Canadians, and Indian signal corps-men with red and yellow cockades in their olive-drab Mont-gomery berets; Chinese merchants with their wives in floppy pajama suits with high collars, and many Vietnamese fam-ilies, the women wearing conical, cream-colored lacquered hats and glazed black or white bell-bottomed trousers. There are also the scrubbed, neatly brushed American secretaries and their beaux, most of them towering a foot or so above the heads of the Lao crowd. Some of the visitors take off their shoes and enter the pagodas where the orange-robed monks are praying, oblivious of the hubbub outside, the light of the votive candles shining on their shaven heads, and the great, darkly golden Buddhas rising in the shadows in the depth of the nave, greater Buddhas dimly visible behind them.

At any *boun,* and on almost any other occasion on which there is a possible excuse for a party, everyone dances the *lamvong.* And in spite of my accumulated incapacity as a ballroom dancer, I found that, eventually, even I could enjoy the revolving *lamvong.* In the Cercle Privé de Vientiane couples revolved around the salon, and in Sayaboury couples revolved around the Governor's porch. At a *boun* they usually revolved on a large, elevated, open-air platform around a sort of Maypole sprouting rose and bluey-white neon bars at the top, and with colored paper streamers running out to the festoons of colored lights strung between the posts that ran around the edge of the floor. Gallants who cannot rest until they dance the *lamvong* buy paper garlands—striped canary and candy pink and apple green, and with a saffron tassel, and present them to the dancing partners who sit at one end of the platform. If the girls are professional taxi dancers and perhaps a little on the light side, it is carefully explained that *they are from across the river,* following the Lao theory that all impropriety must come from Thailand. Often the *bouns* will advertise in the *Lao-Presse:* CAVALIÈRES DE BONNE FAMILLE. They will be, too, very likely from one of the feudal ruling families—delicate little things with tiny waists and high cheekbones, beautiful, and to the stranger, a little impassive looking, shyly flirtatious, yet modest and circumspect. They wear fine gold chains around wrists and neck, and at the throat is a small jade or ivory Buddha edged in gold. They wear their best silk blouses and shawls, woven on the hand loom under every house, their silver belts, and the rich dark skirts bordered with three or four inches of gold or silver trimming, picked out with scarlet and orange, brilliant greens and blues.

When the music for the *lamvong* begins, the girls in their *sins* and the young men in white trousers and aloha shirts begin slowly, gravely, to circle the outside of the floor, two by two, side by side, weaving sinuous patterns with their hands, and with their long slender fingers bent back at impossible angles. In a graceful, measured way, they revolve around one another, advancing, retreating, gesturing, suggesting. It is courtship.

"The lamvong," says Thao Nhouy Abhay in his *Aspects du Pays Lao,* "is the old bacchic carnival dance of our grandfathers spiritualized by the noble breath of the classical theatre." In any case, the traditional drums have been augmented by Laotian violins, mandolins, banjos, and maracas, and as Thao Nhouy notes, the dances now have names like *Hawaï, pak lak, kong ka,* and so on. A young man sings:

> On the back of a water buffalo in the moonlight
> On the back of a water buffalo in the moonlight,
> I see a lovely star. . . .

> My heart trembles . . . Brm, Brm, Brm . . .
> My soul is shaken . . . Chk, Chk, Chk. . . .

And the girl replies:

> Please don't love, don't pursue me,
> I am only the smallest and humblest of reeds,
> You are big, you are fair
> And I am swarthy. . . .

The gestures of the dancers are stylized: a hand over the heart for love, an outstretched arm for far journeys that separate, hands pressed together for prayer. The dancers' faces are blank, or supposed to be, though occasionally one of the young bloods forgets himself and thinks of something funny and giggles or grins. The dancers' feet do a hesitation one-step. And even when the musicians are beside themselves trying to reproduce what they have heard of rock 'n' roll or mambo (you can hear "Oh, Susannah," too), what comes out is indisputably *lamvong* and background music for lotus lovers.

12 THE NEIGHBORS—THAILAND

THE people living in Thailand across the river from Vientiane were not nearly so naughty as the Lao made out. In fact, most of them were Lao. Katay Don Sasorith in his historical-political work *Le Laos* maintains that of Thailand's eighteen million population in 1953, ten million were "Lao," and went on to point out that the various branches of the Thai people spread from North Vietnam west to Burma commonly call one another by that name.

There are now perhaps twenty million subjects of the King of Thailand. This includes a Moslem Malay minority who live in the long, narrow southern pseudopodium which runs down the Malay Peninsula; about three million Chinese who live mostly in the big towns, a number of Cambodians, or Khmer, to the southeast; and in the north, near Burma and China and Laos, many of the tribes who live in all of these countries and who pay little attention to political frontiers.

These with the dominant Thai or Thai-Lao stock are the citizens of Thailand.

Traveling from Vientiane south and west across the green Thai ricelands to Bangkok, the world is the same yet subtly different. It reminded me of driving north as a small boy from Michigan into Ontario with my grandfather when we crossed the Straits of Mackinac and there on the other side, the people looked the same and they spoke the same language, but they had red pillar boxes for letters, and a prime minister instead of a president, and beer with your dinner if you wanted it and were old enough to drink it. There was a familiar mixture of differences and similarities between Thailand and the states of Indochina—especially Laos and Cambodia. Vietnam and Laos and Cambodia were all strongly influenced by France during the last century. The élite of Laos and Cambodia are the children of French culture as well as their own. Thailand remained rather like Ethiopia in her independence: foreign missions and advisers had been around for a long time, but for better or for worse, the country nearly always managed its own affairs.

If Thailand looks abroad, it is to the United States these days, and superimposed on Buddhist Thai culture is a rash of comic books, an erratic effort at television, and batallions of American-trained teachers, nurses, agronomists, and architects. The American orange pop called Green Spot is shipped from the United States in the form of syrup, bottled in a gleaming picture-window plant in Bangkok, and has been celebrated over the local radio with a singing commercial which is nothing more than Thai words set to the song "I Whistle a Happy Tune." This comes from the musical comedy *The King and I,* a Broadway-Hollywood version of *Anna and the King of Siam.* What the Thai have adopted is an American show business view of what life must have been like in Bangkok at the court of King Mongkut.

The officers of the Thai Express Transport Bureau I met on reaching Nongkhai or Udorn all wore suntan uniforms with shoulder boards, high-pressure caps, and winged wheel insignia, looking more like supporters of a South American military junta than people running buses and the trucks and freight cars that carried our supplies. They seemed brisk and citified to us from Laos. The train from Udorn to Bangkok rattles comfortably along through the paddies and the rice mills and the provincial pagodas, with more monks with shaven heads and robes the color of orange ice cream. There are little villages on stilts strung out along the bluffs overlooking the rivers, with a dark-green fringe of palms along the banks; and sometimes in the late afternoons, with the light reflected on the water, I knew why I had always wanted to come to the tropics.

The buses which charge across the Thai landscape in clouds of red dust, like so many frenzied shoeboxes, seat six people abreast on hard wooden benches, with more on top and more hanging from the sides like clusters of grapes. As is usual in Thailand, there are a good many soldiers and military policemen among the passengers who refresh themselves at each stop with the skewers of pineapple, ricecake in banana leaf, and glazed paprika-colored chicken on a stick. Between Udorn and Nong Khai the buses have to stop a number of times at police roadblocks, for in this region are the villages of nearly fifty thousand North Vietnamese refugees, admitted by the postwar pro-Communist Premier Pridi, and still largely under the control of the Vietminh's local security organization; the Thai government would be happy to be rid of them all if only some way could be found to transport them across Laos (reluctant) to Vietnam.

The women planting rice shoots, in the paddies on this side of the border, wear the classical Thai palm-leaf hats, which look like squashed lampshades and sit high off their heads. The small schoolgirls in the towns are barefoot but wear sun helmets. There is a slight Anglo-Saxon gloss: along with the oleo-lithographs of the Buddha and of the bespectacled young King tacked to the walls of the little general stores, with the Chinese-Victorian gilt mirrors painted over with fat pink flowers and birds and characters for prosperity, are stocks of Brooklax and Vicks Medicated Cough Drops; along with Thai tunes I sometimes heard the radios rendering "Jingle Bells." Pedicabs here came from Japan, with snappy nickel mud-guards and red plastic cushions. Of the first five hundred scrawny cats I saw, none was Siamese.

Also living on the west bank of the Mekong across from Vientiane in the region of Udorn are many of the Lao families, with close relatives on both sides of the frontier, who are descendants of the twenty thousand survivors transported to Thailand after the sacking of Vientiane in 1828 by the Thai general Phraya Bodin, who boasted that he left behind him nothing but "land, water and wild beasts." Vientiane, the rich city of pagodas, where the traveler Gerrit van Wusthoff in 1641 found the king carried on a throne of gold and the bonzes "more numerous than the soldiers of the Emperor of Germany," was completely destroyed, its king taken to die in captivity in Bangkok, the Emerald Buddha and the golden Buddha called the Phra Bang, the protector of Laos, taken with him. King Mongkut returned the golden image about ninety years ago to his royal neighbor at Luangprabang, which took its name from the Phra Bang, and there the image may still be seen in the palace of the king, its golden features worn away from the time it once spent lying at the bottom of a river. The Emerald Buddha, or Phra Kéo, remains in Bangkok, where it has become in turn the guardian of Thailand, and there it sits in Wat Phra Kéo, a small image carved of a single piece of dark-green jasper, high on a many-tiered gilt altar, surrounded by ranks of golden Buddhas, its own rich robes changed thrice yearly, for the hot, the "cool," and the rainy seasons. In Vientiane, Vat Phra Kéo has become a museum of antiquities.

The Emerald Buddha, it is supposed, came originally from Ceylon, and its perigrinations followed roughly the path of Buddhism as it was carried to this part of the world from India through Java and Ceylon and Cambodia. Also, the Emerald Buddha reflected the fortunes of war in the struggles between the states. All that is known for certain is that it came to Vientiane from Chieng Mai at the time that that part of northeast Thailand was incorporated into the Kingdom of Lan Xan, after some time as an independent kingdom and buffer state between Thailand and Burma. Ayudhya, the ancient capital of Thailand about forty miles north of Bangkok, was itself completely destroyed about two hundred years ago during the long and inconclusive wars with the Burmese.

Thailand was known as Siam until 1939, when it changed its name to Thailand, then back to Siam in 1945, and to Thailand again in 1949. As this is written, it is officially Thailand. Whatever the name, it is twice the size of Laos, with anywhere from five to twenty times as many inhabitants (depending on how many Lao there really are). It is infinitely more cosmopolitan, and with a certain disarming cheerfulness which most foreign observers lay partly to its survival as an independent nation during the colonial struggles in southeast Asia. This, many further feel, is in part due to Thailand's adroit trimming of its sails to prevalent political winds, and to general Thai acceptance, so far, of imperfection in government and man. At any rate, as Faubion Bowers remarks in his delightful study *Theatre in the East,* "Whatever else may be said about Thailand . . . it is aesthetically mature as a country."

Bangkok fulfills this promise, though the first impression of many visitors is that they are about to be killed. They emerge from the international airport at Donmuang, about forty-five minutes out of town, where the big planes of Air France, BOAC, KLM, Pan American, and the others take off for the great cities of the world. Most of them bound eastward fly over Laos, but it is doubtful whether the passengers are aware of it.

The tired travelers, safely arrived in Bangkok, are now faced with the most exhilarating voyage I know this side of the Indianapolis Speedway. Paris traffic is nothing. Neither are the chasm-prone bus drivers of South and Central America. The easiest way to describe the ride from the airport to town is to say that only once in two dozen trips have I been in or out without seeing a wreck. "Look that car," said Praesert, the stocky, cheerful taxi driver who worked the line outside the Oriental Hotel, one of the first times I rode in. The car was crumpled up against a tree. The last time I rode out he told me sorrowfully that the evening before, a bus had plunged into a canal with sixty passengers, all of whom drowned.

The canals are called *klongs.* A network of them crisscrosses the city, and beside the road there are sampans poling along, and little wooden bridges, and people sitting on their front stoops washing the baby, the dog, or their sarongs, brushing their teeth or filling their earthenware water jars. Nearing town, the traffic becomes heavier and more confused. There were times when I was reminded of both Manhattan's cross-town theater traffic and the Dodgem at Coney Island. Instead of the collections of mass-production pottery gnomes and cranes and the gorgeous mirror balls on pedestals offered by the lawn ornament vendors along the American highways, the roadside vendors here are surrounded with mass-production spired Buddhist monuments and the ochre and cherry and pea-green versions of the homes for family spirits that look like birdhouses on poles. Beyond the trees that line the road are the swooping, overlapping, shimmering golden roofs of the pagodas. The road is choked with crazy buses and military trucks and the Thai rickshas called *samlors* ("three-wheels") skating back and forth like water bugs. The cycle *samlors* pedal briskly along, bunches of paper flowers tied to the handlebars, and the motor *samlors* cut through traffic with a nonchalance that would scare the wits out of their passengers if they were not half asphyxiated by the exhaust of the motorcycle directly ahead of them, and in no condition to notice or think about anything else. In town this happy, suicidal throng is joined by ancient, open-air yellow trolley cars which run on a single track down one side of New Road so that half of the time they are bucking the oncoming stream.

The Oriental Hotel where I liked to stay is a handsome, jalousied gingerbread wedding cake looking out over the Chao Phraya River that winds through the center of the city. I was reminded that I hadn't yet left the tropics by the faint yelps of the geckos and the swarms of mosquitoes rising from the toilet bowl. The climate is hot and humid—my original impression that Bangkok was cool held true only for that first day I passed through on my way out of Saigon. Ordinarily you swelter. The new hotels and the elegant shops are as air-conditioned as the petroleum sheikhdoms of Arabia, but I preferred the Oriental, and not one of its air-conditioned rooms, though the others there were becoming increasingly rare, to see and hear the life on Bangkok's river. At night lights on the freighters anchored in midstream turn the old rust pots into floating palaces. I wondered if any of my old untrammeled shipmates during my brief and inglorious career as an undergraduate merchant seaman ever made this port. You can hear the cable winding on the donkey engines, the anchor chain coming up, the creaking of the blocks, and the soft, persistent putt-putting of the launches moving up and down the river. Big, fat-bellied, square-sterned junks chug slowly along, and all day long, taxi sampans scull back and forth across the wide river. Past the masts and cargo booms and white superstructures of the freight ships you can see on the far shore a line of low buildings, weathered gray wood with sienna rust patches on their corrugated tin roofs. On some of the warehouses is faded camouflage, left over from the war when Bangkok had been bombed by the Allies.

Outside your balcony at the Oriental, the handsome russet sea eagles swoop, and the sea gulls skreek. Inside, there is a blast of hot air as you walk along the corridor past the air-conditioning boxes stuck to the rooms which they cool. In the patio of the Oriental grow slender palms like gently curved thirty-foot pencils topped with a mop, and the restaurant on a great open veranda looks out on the lively river, but the hotel's Bamboo Bar where I sometimes ate dinner in Bangkok was as far removed from the city as a cosy corner in the Antarctic. Dimly lit, with the Bamboobar Combo playing piano, sax, drums, and maracas, and little lamps with Cam-

bodian elephants, gods, and demons picked out on the parch-
ment shades, all shining down on impeccable napery ornamented at mid-table with fern leaves and flat roses—this was
all very far away from Vientiane, and all in great part due to
the skill of the manager, Germaine Krull, a strong, warm,
decided and delightful woman in middle years who had
worked for a woman's magazine in Paris, done a hitch in the
French underground in North Africa, and who was the cre-
ator of a book of pictures of Chieng Mai, the old Lao-Thai
capital in the north of what is now Thailand, and where
she keeps a home. Her lieutenant is a solid, bright, jolly Thai
named Chalerm Kaukhan, who presides over the Bamboo
Bar and can chat easily with a customer while his eye is on
every waiter in the room. Between them, they run a really
good hotel, a rare and wonderful skill that is as specialized
as diamond cutting or running a circus.

I run on about the Oriental and Bangkok perhaps because
of the bright lights. Anything in Thailand was apt to dazzle
anyone from Laos. It was to this city that the Lao Issara
refugees came in 1946, to work as hotel dishwashers and
weavers and pamphleteers during the days when they were
struggling to win complete independence from France. There
were during this period some ten thousand Lao refugees in
the country. This and Lao insistence on running their own
country after the war, the record of Lao troops harassing the
French, and later with the French, smashing the Vietminh's
attempt to set up a permanent base in south Laos—all this
suggests that the outsider's traditional picture of the Lao as
a charming child of nature now needs a little qualification.
It is unlikely that the Lao, or the Thai or the Cambodians or
Indians or Chinese or anyone else for that matter, are im-
mutable, any more than ideas. After all, it is not so many

years since the modest, democratic Swedes were the Vikings, pillaging, burning, and raping, and the prayer went up in English churches: "O God, deliver us from the Norsemen."

To return to Thailand and Bangkok, there is still a good deal of the traditional Thai mixed in with all the advertising and Western dress and television in the hotel lobby. The façade of the Oriental facing the river looks like a set for a musical comedy about the tropics in the 1890s: a lawn like a rich, dark putting green leads to an entrance guarded by great shallow stone chalices filled with flowers and two neo-classical bronze maidens holding electric torches shaped like the Olympic flame; wrought-iron railings and high folding French doors, windows capped with fanlights give into cool, dark, high-ceilinged rooms; the whole is surmounted by a marvelous Dutch gable like a falsefront second story, with the name of the hotel spelled out just below in large, turn-of-the-century, ornate, high-button lettering. The streets on the landward side of the hotel are lined with bareheaded vendors squatting by the roadside, and wearing the Thai version of the sarong. This is in defiance of the government's announcement a few years ago that honest Thai citizens would forego sarongs and wear hats. I noticed that the laundry list at the hotel included

> Sarong
> Kimono
> Stay
> Diaper
> Turban
> Watch Chain

The turbans were presumably those of visiting Indians or an occasional resident Sikh who, in Bangkok as in Hong Kong, specialize in the night-watchman and bank-guarding business; they run to fierce mustaches, awesome pot bellies, and dhotis, and they seem to spend most of their time sitting down.

Other men mostly wear Western sack suits. Women wear anything from slacks and shorts to pedal pushers and the garment industry's Balinese uplift. They are a handsome brown, with flat faces, high cheekbones, everted lips, favor a poodle's coiffure, and are perpetually smiling. They tend to be small and chubby, with taut little tummies and rears set off with flounces and bustles and such. Simple blouses are in fashion. They like red. The men just look like men.

The street lights on the lamp posts on Rajadamnoen Avenue are carried by the bosomatic heavenly musicians called Kinaras, wearing the traditional tapered Thai diadem, half jungle fowl, half celestial chorus girl. The postal employees at the GPO around the corner from the Oriental wear latterday military suntans with shoulder straps and red, white, and gold braid, but they do their sums on abaci, sell stamps across which march elephants bearing kings under ceremonial parasols, or sail the helmeted, hawklike bird-man garuda, who is the steed of the god Vishnu.

Bangkok offers a remarkable assortment of entertainment. There is Thai foot-fighting at the arena, where the boxers are accompanied by a band that tootles and crashes as they kick, and where each man dances a little ritual pantomime before the fight begins. You can visit the municipal snake farm where antivenin is made, and where during the disastrous flood of 1942 all the cobras and kraits swam away. There is a magnificent collection of bronzes in the National Library and Museum—a number of heads and figures of the Buddha as fine as anything to be seen in Laos or Cambodia—housed in what used to be the palace of that curious Thai institution, the Second King. In the Thieves Market you can buy moonstones and star saphires, star rubies, zircons, and antiquities from the tiny, broken Buddha heads collected by the juvenile black market in the ruins of Ayudhya to bronze sun drums from the Thai-Lao frontier country and big bronze *hongs,* used as pagoda roof ornaments until the bird fell into disfavor because of its Burmese origins (the people here have not forgotten the Burmese destruction of Ayudhya, their capital for four hundred years). In the center of town is the Thai Silk Company, surrounded by a flock of imitators, where an American architect named James Thompson who had been in Thailand with the OSS during the war came back to foster a Thai silk industry. He introduced better looms and good dyes that don't run, and is a happy colorist who did such cheerful, bright things with traditional Thai patterns that soon his stoles, cummerbunds, scarves, blouses, and sport shirts were found hung on well-dressed Thai and foreigner alike, and his four-in-hand Thai ties were being sold for $10 and $12.50 each in New York. A good many of the Lao refugees worked making Thai silk.

There is a rich selection of foreign and Thai films on view in Bangkok, and the most popular of all the Thai productions are silent. Customarily they are shot in color, but in sixteen millimeter rather than the standard commercial thirty-five. Known to the American information people as Adam & Eve shows, the Thai films depend on the services of male and female teams of two who between them can take any part yet written, including incidental noises for poultry, wild beasts, and creaking doors, and with modulation to suggest characters turning, advancing, or receding. The Adam & Eve duos work through mikes from the projection booth or just behind the screen, and it is a tribute to Thai tenacity that the Adam & Eve shows play the largest houses in town, and steadily outdraw Hollywood.

With the three million or so Chinese in Thailand, there is a good choice of Cantonese or Mandarin opera, an art form I still don't understand: the sets are double-bourgeois ancient Chinese-Grand-Rapids, with curly cloud effects and dragon motifs while you wait. The acting is the broadest I've ever seen outside the Yiddish Art Theatre. The Chinese principals, in rich costumes with sleeves that flap and beards hanging from the lower lip like a fringe, stagger with passion, recoil, double-take, and go bug-eyed when moved. The music goes clop-clop, bok-bok, whang, bang, crash and rattle. The plots are no more illogical than those of Hollywood.

A leading American daily paper printed a report recently that Bangkok has become the world's capital of pornographic films. They are there, at least according to the touts in the street, but this strikes me as a dubiously absolute statistic. Much easier to verify are the opium dens which are on the regular tourist circuit. One down the street was open twenty-four hours a day, and resembled nothing so much as a ramshackle warehouse. I went along one day with one of the senior nurses from Johns Hopkins, thinking I would be in safe hands. Splashy red characters on milk glass announced the equivalent of "Opium Den" in Chinese. This was perfectly legal, for opium was still a government monopoly, controlled by the police, and a flurry of exhortations and announcements that the government was to abandon its interest in narcotics had to be postponed because of the needs of internal revenue. So I found myself with a nurse in attendance reclining on a porcelain pillow in a cubicle, smoking two pipes of opium in an opium den. This was equivalent to two good, sucking, bubbly whiffs, after an attendant had prepared the pipe each time, turning a little nubbin of opium at the end of a needle in the flame of a small, thick, cut-glass lamp before inserting the smoking gum in the long pipe. I waited for something to happen. Nothing happened. The nurse seemed to be in complete control of herself, though she declined more than one pipe. A number of infants, several small boys, and an assortment of neighbors gathered in front of the cubicle to see what the foreign devils were up to. Nothing happened. Then there was a hiss, a couple of fingers poked through the split bamboo matting separating our cubicle from the next one. This was followed by a nose, and a mysterious Oriental voice said, "I speak English, I lived in Chicago."

My favorite among the delights of Bangkok has always been the early morning cruise through the *klongs*. When the mists are still on the river, you can pick up a launch by the Oriental's back lawn and head out to the Floating Market through the shipping of the Chao Phraya: round-roofed freight sampans, a little like flattened covered wagons, heavy with charcoal and grain, Pepsi-Cola and Chinese cabbage; Chris-Craft, ferry boats, firewood barges, high-pooped junks; Caltex, Shell, and Mobiloil barges; a gunboat with a garuda figurehead; customs boats and police boats and what I take to be navy boats with white elephant flags on their jack staffs. Small boys, ducking and laughing, hitch rides on the launches as they go by, and come within inches of being run down. Commuters living on the outskirts of town catch their bus boats to work.

In the Floating Market there is an early morning nautical traffic jam, with vendors wearing the usual lampshades poling along and peddling breadfruit, mangoes, bananas, and spiky, brownish-green durians, selling potted plants and small trees, carrying chickens to market in loosely-woven wicker baskets each large enough to carry three men inside. Some of the boats carry offerings of little bouquets of flowers and smoking joss sticks and scraps of chartreuse or magenta chiffon fluttering at bow or stern. Boats carry their wares from house to house on the riverbank, lined with flame-of-the-forest trees and coconut palms, clumps of bamboo and lush, high grass. All of the houses on piles have their own little landings. There are marine filling stations, and the Chinese and Thai shops sell rope and toothpaste and household effects to their boating customers. The tourists in the launches snap pictures, and move on to see Wat Arun, the Temple of the Dawn, from the river, and the boat house at the Royal Landing where the King's barges are kept. They lie beached there, long and lonely in the shadows now, with the nagas and garudas and monkey warriors on their prows, while below them the popeyed little mud skippers skitter over the mangrove roots at low tide. The largest barge is about a hundred and seventy feet long, covered with gold leaf and mosaic in colored glass. It took 150 soldiers to man it with golden paddles, with a singing coxswain and a chief officer, and, of course, plenty of parasols.

From the river as from the road there are pagoda roofs everywhere, green and orange tiles, with gilded eaves. Not so many proportionately as in Vientiane, for at that rate I calculate that Greater Bangkok would need more than nine thousand pagodas. But there are three hundred of them anyway, and each morning the monks with shaven heads and saffron robes and begging bowls humbly ask for alms along the roads. Away from the monastery, they simply stick their open parasols in the earth, cover them with circular mosquito nets, and sleep on the ground until the faithful bring them food in the morning. They look fine in the water taxis, a couple of splotches of orange against the slaty Chao Phraya, with dabs of black or dark red over their heads where they carry their parasols.

There are shrines on poles in the water and more shrines on the shore, and the tallest of them all is the Temple of the Dawn, a great spire capped with the trident of Siva, and sprouting the trunks of the three-headed elephants on which rides the god Indra. The temples are surrounded with lion dogs with stone balls in their mouths, with wispy-bearded sages, and other statues brought from China, they are guarded by terrible giants with upturned tushes like those of a wild boar, and they sparkle with the hundreds of thousands of bits of Venetian gold glass and of Japanese and Chinese crockery systematically broken and rearranged to form flower mosaics.

It would take many weeks and many visits to Bangkok to come to know the Temple of the Dawn and the Temple of the Emerald Buddha, the lovely marble chapel at Wat Benchaminbopit, the block-long Reclining Buddha at Wa Po, whose feet are carved with scenes from his own life, the Standing Buddha and Wat Indra Vihan, and all the rest. And everywhere, on the towers and in the gardens, are the tiny temple bells tinkling in the breeze.

For those who begin to get pagoda feet from tramping around the temples, there is a round of lighter distractions: Thai *bouns* are full of Thai music and side shows, dart boards, hoop-la, bingo, and *lamvong*, which here becomes the *ramwong*, a little jazzier and to my mind not so graceful as its Lao cousin. Anyway, it's fun, and intending visitors can *ramwong* with taxi girls with names like The Cobra and The Tiger in a ballroom on the top floor of a good Chinese restaurant called Hoi Thien Lao, a place much favored by pilots and other wandering foreigners in town.

Of all the Thai entertainments, the theater is the thing. There are shadow shows, becoming rare now, and the classical, stylized ballet, the masked pantomime and the dance drama, and the popular, representational modern Thai drama. In form and origin Thai theater is close to that in Burma and Cambodia and Laos, and because of the number and accessibility of the playhouses and the growing body of interpretive and critical literature in English, Bangkok is probably the best place in this interdependent region to learn something of the dance and drama of, say, Laos and Cambodia, and the common background of them all. The Royal Lao Ballet at the court in Luangprabang, as it happens, was founded on a troupe of entertainers brought in recent years from Thailand, and the Thai dance-drama called *lakon* was brought to Thailand with a troupe of Cambodian palace dancers kidnapped in a body a couple of hundred years ago for the Thai king's seraglio.

The stories are likely to be the same wonderful old tales from the *Ramayana,* about Rama and his beautiful wife Sita, abducted by the green-faced, polycephalic demon King of Ceylon, Ravana, whom the Thai usually call Ten Necks; about the struggles to win Sita back with the aid of the "distinguished monkey warrior" Hanuman. Faubion Bowers gives this synopsis of the plot of one of the *khon* pantomimes:

> "The pyrotechnics of the Khon play I am describing begin when Hanuman is alone on the stage and, after many characteristic acts like rolling on the ground, scratching himself for lice, and monkey-like frolicking over the stage, sets out on his hazardous journey to the nether world. In an attempt to block him en route, a magician creates several obstruc-

tions. First, an enormous elephant of gray cloth, with two men to act as the fore and hind feet, walks out from underneath the stage and romps around the grass before the audience. Hanuman grapples with him and kills him barehanded. Then there is an explosion of gunpowder and the rocky crag off to one side is filled with flames made by off-stage attendants rapidly fanning bright red strips of silk. Hanuman heroically lifts a huge papier-mâché boulder and throws it over the fire to smother it. Then follows a horde of enormous paper mosquitoes, the size of crows, slowly pulled along wire suspended across the top of the stage between the two trees. They attack Hanuman, but he fights some of them off and crushes the others with his hands. Finally Hanuman reaches a lotus pond which miraculously appears on stage. There he finds a young guardian at the gates of Hell who is half-fish, half-monkey. Hanuman recognises him as his own son, the product of an early indiscretion with a mermaid, but in order to prove his identity to the boy, he performs the great "miracle of Hanuman," that of emitting the moon and the stars by a single yawn. The sacred magic music sounds. Suddenly the moon and stars appear, bright and shining in the air. Finally, Hanuman divines that the quickest route to Rama in the nether world is down the stem of a lotus, and the Khon is concluded as he leaps headfirst off the stage into the petals of a giant lotus in front."

In these stories the gestures of the actors and the dancers are all-important. Some are obvious to outsiders, all are familiar to the audience: pointing the finger and stamping the foot for anger, holding the brow for sorrow or wiping away tears with the left hand, crossed arms rhythmically pressing the chest for agitation or bereavement, forefingers drawn along the line of the mouth and upwards for happiness. There is a whole alphabet of dance mime, originally with sixty-four letters but now reduced to nineteen which Mr. Bowers lists as:

Salute to the Gods (the obeisance movement of the hand placed together in front of the face with which all dances begin in Thailand)
Preliminary Movement
Prohm (Brahma) with the Four Faces
Tucking in the Garland's Tassels
Stag Walking in the Forest
Swan in Flight
Kinnara Walking around the Cave
Putting the Lady to Sleep
Bee's Caress
The Cockatoo
The Little Hill as High as the Shoulder
Mekala Playing with her Precious Jewel
The Peacock Dances
Wind Swaying the Plantain Leaf
Transformation
Wedded Love
Changing the Posture
Fish Playing in the Ocean
Pra Naray (Vishnu) Hurling His Discus

There is also elaborately stylized mood music instantly familiar to the audience—crying music, exit music, copulatory music, and almost any kind of music you can think of.

Rama I, the founder of the present Thai dynasty, in the late eighteenth and early nineteenth centuries wrote the first of the modern Thai plays based on the *Ramayana*. His son Rama II wrote many more, including the popular tale of the poor man who won the rich man's daughter by killing the crocodile king who had carried her off. Rama VI, who reigned until 1925, wrote even more plays, including some in English and French. There is now in Bangkok a strong classical Thai theatrical revival, owing largely to the Chulalongkorn University (named after the son of King Mongkut) Department of Fine Arts whose Silkaporn Theatre is more popular than American films, and makes more money than anybody.

All of this is wonderful and exciting, but if I could have done so, I would have headed north at the first opportunity to the teak country, where the great elephants work. They are still an important factor in the Thai economy. It was Rama IV, Anna's King Mongkut, who courteously sent Abraham Lincoln an offer of Thai elephants to roam the American jungle as a perpetual supply of draft animals. Mr. Lincoln answered that unfortunately the United States did not "reach a latitude so low as to favor the multiplication of the elephant," adding that so far steam had proved "our best and most efficient agent of transportation."

Also in the north live the Lao-Thai and the same tribespeople, the silver-collared Meo and the turbaned Lu and all the others that spread across that ethnic no man's land of south China, northern Laos, Burma, and Thailand. On the one occasion when I did travel up through Chieng Mai, Chieng Rai, and Chieng Sen in Thailand on my way to Houei Sai just down the Mekong and nearby in Laos, it was delightful—except for a little tension along the Burmese border where Thai authorities had just confiscated twenty tons of opium which smugglers were trying to put through nonofficial channels. Northern Thailand is so completely Lao that I felt I was at home.

13 CAMBODIA: THE PRINCE'S COUNTRY

"CAMBODIA" has always sounded to me like childhood stories before bedtime—something about a distant land of pagodas and painted elephants, and on the swooping roofs of the palaces little bells that tinkled in the wind. A Prince of Cambodia would surely be a personage in a ballet or a fairy tale, with magical powers and curly shoes and a costume of emerald silk shot with gold. Even after I had come to live in Indochina and had heard the temple bells, just the phrase "The Kingdom of Cambodia" was strangely evocative. Now that finally I have seen the kingdom, I suspect that it is not far from all those things I dreamed. Except that now there are some new characters: fairy godmothers in the shape of Eastern and Western plenipotentiaries bearing gifts. And there is always the Prince.

The Prince is Norodom Sihanouk, a plump and nimble young man, born on October 31, 1922, who was crowned King of Cambodia in 1941, three days before his nineteenth birthday. In 1955 as a veteran statesman in his mid-thirties, he relinquished the throne in order to become Prime Minister and to plunge into politics without kingly limitations. In a special Cambodian and Sihanoukian way, the crown went backwards to his father and mother, Norodom Suramarit and Kossamak Nearireak, who thus became Sihanouk's successors though they had not been his predecessors.

According to Rand McNally, Sihanouk's country is a land of some sixty-nine thousand square miles, the size of Oklahoma. Cambodia's resemblance to Oklahoma ends right there. Like their neighbors the Lao and the Thai and the Vietnamese, the Cambodians eat rice. Cambodia is an aquatic, or at the driest, an amphibious country. Like much of Thailand and southern India, the country is a green and silver quilt of paddies and irrigation ditches, with bright pale-green shoots piercing the mirror of the wet fields, with metallic blue-and-green kingfishers skimming above the surface of the water, with the tractable and moistly gleaming water buffaloes carrying small children, and the wading figures, sarongs tucked up, bent over planting or harvesting the rice. There is water everywhere. The Mekong which began life in the Tibetan mountains has here become a great highway, and has as its storage basin during the rainy season a large lake called the Tonle Sap, with the result that from May to December the tributary Tonle Sap River runs northwest, and for the rest of the year, southeast.

It is a country a little like the Everglades, with ponds and ditches, marshes and savannahs. The moat that runs around the great temple of Angkor Vat is two and a half miles long and filled with fish and turtles, and in the bad old days, crocodiles. In the rainy season Cambodians in their graceful, slender pirogues go boating from field to field and from house to house, perched above the flood waters on high stilts, like those in Laos. Canals and reflecting pools are choked with pink and white lotuses and water lilies and lavender water hyacinths, and among the egrets and cormorants and pelicans and raucous black ravens, squadrons of dragon flies dart above the water, and there are great white herons wading in the fields, their long necks and heads sticking stiffly up above the green rice sprouts like so many angular umbrella handles.

The countryside inhabited by most of the 4½ million Cambodians stretches flat and peaceful to the horizon, with lonely little hills now and then, and a couple of ranges to the south and east called the Elephants and the Cardamoms. Throughout the country there are patches of banana trees and coconut palms, light-green bamboo, high-buttressed silk-cotton trees, and mangroves in the water of the bayous. There are banyans, pomegranates, sandalwood, aloes, and pepper which the Cambodians insist is the best in the world. As in the neighboring countries, the elephant is a domestic animal, and Cambodians also like to ride cows. Along the roads creak the high-wheeled oxcarts covered with rattan hoods, long wagon tongues curling before them like nagas' tails, and dogs trotting beneath the carts in the shade. Most of the other traffic is on foot: boy bonzes from the pagodas, country people with tousled black gypsy hair and checkered emerald-and-magenta sarongs, or more likely with rather indifferent European pants and shirt, with perhaps a black-and-white-checked scarf thrown over one shoulder.

Cambodia lies south of China and east of India, or more closely, just to the south of Thailand and Laos and to the west of Vietnam. It is an hour by air from Saigon to the Cambodian capital of Phnom-Penh, and a couple of hours on the daily plane from Bangkok; once a week the famous Stratoliner of Air Laos makes the run from Vientiane to Phnom-Penh. It is a fascinating, an exciting country. Visiting Cambodia for me was a curious sort of home-coming, for here, in the exile of Fa Ngoum, Laos had been born, here were the origins of much of Lao-Thai religion and the closely related architecture, music, and dancing.

Three things strike one arriving in Cambodia for the first time, and he will seldom be allowed to forget them until he leaves: first is the glory of the ancient Khmer Empire symbolized by Angkor Vat and its use as an emblem of the renascent Khmer in their newly independent state led by Prince Sihanouk. Next, this country of the temple dancers seems to have become a major arena of competing politico-economic philosophies, expressed in terms of foreign aid. If Laos has perhaps the greatest number of foreign aid dollars per person of any country I know of, then Cambodia has the most sorts of aid. Among the Cambodian pagodas now are the emissaries of American aid, Russian aid, Communist Chinese aid, French aid, Colombo Plan aid, and United Nations aid. Czechoslovak, Polish, and Japanese aid have been offered, and accepted in principle. Competition is keen, and not only between East and West. Aid has been offered by India, leader of the uncommitted nations.

The third, the most singular, and I believe the most important fact of life in the new Khmer Kingdom is the Prince. His Royal Highness Samdech Preah Upayuvareach Norodom Sihanouk is a master of the unexpected. He throws off ideas like sparks from a pinwheel. His highly unorthodox approach to world affairs has often baffled other players in the game. When, in 1953, still king, he felt the French were not handing over the reigns of power with sufficient dispatch, he took off for Bangkok and the Cambodian provinces, and refused to come back until the French gave in. A year later, when Britain, Russia, Communist China, and the other interested powers at Geneva were ready to seal the agreement which put an end to the fighting in Indochina, Sihanouk's delegates at the last moment refused to sign until Cambodia's special demands—the right to rearm and to contract alliances—were met. After five hours the powers gave in, and Cambodia emerged with a more favorable settlement than either Laos or Vietnam.

The Western press has been intrigued by the fact that Norodom Sihanouk can play the saxophone, and has composed a "Cambodian Suite" recorded by André Kostelanetz. *Time* happily reported that the ex-king kept a stable of race horses and ceremonial elephants, and a "personal troupe of 50 dancing girls." Sihanouk, said *Time*, liked to play sax in his own orchestra, and had produced his own films, in one of which he had appeared as a mad scientist manufacturing zombies. Perhaps it is just the contrast with our own comparatively staid statesmen: it is difficult to imagine John Foster Dulles in public playing so much as a ukelele. But in this part of the world such good cheer is not odd. Not only is the king of Thailand a jazz musician, but Sihanouk's father, King Suramarit, plays the flute and clarinet, and has written "Cambodian Sketches," while the Prince's mother has organized the Royal Cambodian Ballet, presumably the troupe that the excited reporter had in mind.

This preoccupation with the Cambodian Prince's mercurial and theatrical personality may have obscured the fact that—however unpredictable—he is one of the most creative political strategists now at work. A great admirer of Jawaharlal Nehru and his political philosophy of nonalignment (there is reciprocity), Sihanouk has fashioned his own special brand of Cambodian nonalignment—personal, pragmatic, or perhaps intuitive, but at any rate with the initiative of surprise, extreme suppleness, and not a little subtlety. He has parlayed his own adroitness and the rivalry of the powers, his geographical position and the political currents of our emergent nationalist and anticolonial times into a power in world affairs that far exceeds the almanac's statistics on Cambodia's area, population, and gross national produce.

Since he turned the crown over to his parents, Sihanouk has been Prime Minister off and on, Foreign Minister, and *de facto* Minister of the Interior, in charge of police and pagodas. Outside the palace grounds stands a billboard that looks as though it had been painted by an experienced side show banner artist: there is a portrait of the Prince at the top, flanked by the assorted national flags of his hosts, and below, a red-and-blue map showing his voyages to India, Japan, Communist China, the Philippines, Spain, Poland, Russia, Czechoslovakia, Yugoslavia, and Austria.

The Prince's travels have been broadening. In a perceptive interview circulated by the wire service NANA and headed:

EX-KING IN PARIS TO GIVE THE FRENCH A "GOOD SHAKING UP"

the correspondent Bernard Kaplan reported that "this moon-faced, boyish ex-king of Cambodia" had been described as "what Nehru would be if he had had French tutors," and went on to conclude that "the Cambodian Prince is no dilettante dabbling in affairs of state, but a shrewd, strong-willed politician. To their sorrow, the French have found that he usually means exactly what he says. By a skillful mixture of pressure and cajolery, Sihanouk wrested virtually every important political concession from the French before the war ended."

On his return from Peking in 1956, when Americans in Phnom-Penh anticipated a few friendly words as neutralist counterbalance, the home-coming Prince treated the crowd at the airport meadow with a scathing description of US aid to his country as little more than "fancy automobiles and refrigerators." This was the period known to Americans in Cambodia as "the time of troubles." Sihanouk in another speech said, "This is certainly not the place for an American aid program of the flashy type, nor for journalists with big slogans." About the same time, the Prince made the unvarnished summing up to his people: "I must first of all proclaim that we are not able now to give up American aid *without falling into the orbit of the Communist powers,* which would mean the end of our neutrality, and probably of our independence" (italics the Prince's).

Whatever his momentary belittling of American aid projects, Sihanouk's alarming interpretation of the American position obliged Secretary of State Dulles to go on record saying that the United States is not opposed to Cambodian neutrality; and Vice-President Nixon's curt comment in Karachi that any nation which accepted Communist aid with "no strings attached" ran the risk, not of strings, but of a "rope tied around its neck" had to be qualified quickly with the reassurance that American aid would be forthcoming "if it would help that nation become stronger and independent, even though it took Communist aid." This was quickly put to test in Cambodia.

Yet Sihanouk welcomed the Chinese aid-and-trade delegation which came to Phnom-Penh after his visit to Peking with a stern warning to the visitors not to meddle in Cambodian politics. On his return from Moscow his airfield speech was full of praise for his French and American friends, and during the Cambodian tour of Chou En-lai, when some American correspondents asked him what he would do if United States aid were discontinued, Sihanouk said flatly, "To lose their help would be a disaster." Sihanouk has the balancer's flair. He is politically tantalizing and provocative. But it is well to remember that even in 1953 he was saying clearly that neither Khmer priests nor people wanted Communism nor that curious sort of independence in which the North Vietnamese and the Russians were their masters. More recently the Prince has published in the weekly *Réalités Cambodgiennes* a series of articles warning his compatriots against the efforts of the miniscule Cambodian Communist party, with a good deal of help from outside, to woo students (free books, scholarships, trips to the Promised Land); the peasants ("the Prince is our friend"); the Buddhist bonzes ("The Throne obstructs the Church," which would otherwise run the country and lead everyone to that happiness foreseen by the Buddha); and the intellectuals and the general public with a subsidized press with stories about the encouragement of all religions in Communist lands, and all the other familiar themes.

A latter-day device and one that flourished in the pages of the pro-Sihanouk *Réalités* itself, in the pen pals column called *Chaine de l'Amitié,* was the use of Esperanto for propaganda purposes. As opposed to their tactics in 1950 when only the son of Dr. Lazarus Zamenhof, the inventor of the international language, was allowed out of Eastern Europe as a lonely representative of the Communist world at the international Esperanto conclave at Copenhagen, now the air was suddenly full of Esperantist pen pals in Bulgaria, Poland, North Vietnam, and Russia who wanted to exchange stamps and post cards and make young friends in Cambodia. A Soviet philologist offered to correspond in Esperanto, French, English, Khmer, Burmese, or Malay. When the editor discovered that the names and addresses of all the young Cambodians whose announcements appeared were being sent directly to a certain Mr. Van Kine of the Moscow Esperanto Office, he called a halt.

In a passionate address to his own political party, the Sangkum, Prince Sihanouk put it as plainly as any nonaligned statesman could do: "The Communist party is beginning to cause trouble. I know that they would like to cut my throat, but if the moment comes to die or be imprisoned, we shall know that we have not betrayed our country. . . . Many countries have not believed in the mortal danger of world Communism, and then, when the evidence became clear to them, it was too late and impossible for them to come to their senses. Look at Hungary!" Sihanouk's stand and the similar stiffening of the new government of Malaya, the growing acceptability of President Diem's South Vietnam, and other straws in the Southeast Asian wind should have their repercussions in Laos as the kingdom tries to work out some sort of modus vivendi with its rough neighbors in China and North Vietnam.

The Prince's capital claims a third of a million souls, but it has the feeling of a provincial town in the south of France, drowsing on a hot summer's day, full of history and old families and flowering trees along shady avenues. On a wet night the ribbed buggy tops of the pedicabs shine in the light of the street lamps. The rural elephants and rhinoceroses and tigers seem far away, but there are still little reminders that

Cambodia is in the tropics: the soggy heat; the guavas and litchis in the market; the small boy flying an irridescent green scarab at the end of a thread; a pair of pet gibbons whooping in somebody's back yard. The chewing-gum-pink terazzo porte-cochère of the Cambodian National Bank is supported by stylized many-headed cobras.

The Prince's fellow subjects are a mild and peaceable people. They range in color from light olive to deepest chestnut, and their faces run from the bland, rounded Javanese mask familiar throughout Southeast Asia to the lean, dark, quick raggle-taggle-gypsy-oh look more reminiscent of southern India than the rest of this peninsula. They are a pastoral and village people, like their neighbors. They strike visitors as fond of jokes, as often amorous, sometimes ironical:

> The refuge of the scholar is science,
> of the rhinoceros, the bush, of the tiger,
> the forest, of the elephant, the marsh,
> of the brave man, the brawl, and of the drinker,
> the glass.

and they pray:

> Please, little genies,
> and you big ones, too,
> I beg you,
> Won't you come down out of the mountains
> And enjoy yourselves?

As with most people in this older, more anciently civilized part of the world, the origins of the Khmer are hazy. Nobody even knows the local name of the state which flourished during the first five hundred years of the Christian era on the marshy, monsoonal Mekong delta on the South China Sea.

The Chinese called it Fu-Nan, and one of their anonymous dynastic historians reported: "The men are all ugly and black. Their hair is curly. They go naked and barefoot." Buddhist pilgrims passed through here, and Indian and Arab voyagers touched the coast, but by the seventh century the outside world had forgotten where Fu-Nan was. All that is known now is that the state became a vassal to its own ex-vassal, Chenla, or Kambuja, and this in turn became the great Khmer kingdom founded by Jayavarman II in 802 atop Mount Mahendra. The following 650 years of Cambodia's Angkor or classical Khmer period saw a civilization which was a considerable maritime power, and which ruled over most of the rest of the Indochinese peninsula, including large parts of what are now Vietnam, Thailand, and Laos. It was a complex, highly organized society, skilled at warfare and at sculpture. It was based on slave labor. Angkor and the other temple cities around Siemreap are as extraordinary as anything left by the Maya or the Egyptians or the Greeks. The Khmer were militant, but wars play a relatively small part in known Cambodian history, which is mostly the story of the development of their art and architecture.

For about half a century now, the Sunday supplements and the travel folders have been insisting that the splendid ruins of Angkor Vat are those of a lost civilization whose inhabitants disappeared without a trace. What really happened was very simple—they moved to Phnom-Penh. Following a defeat by the Thai in 1431, the Khmer king and most of his surviving subjects moved south to the site of the new capital, where they have been ever since. The country's boundaries shrank to their present size. Cambodia became a French protectorate about a hundred years ago, more or less independent in 1949, and completely so in 1953.

According to Lawrence Palmer Briggs' *Ancient Khmer Empire*, historical continuity is better established for ancient Cambodia than it is for Egypt. The nine hundred-odd inscriptions found around Angkor give an unbroken line of kings from the early ninth to the mid-fourteenth centuries.

The family of Sihanouk traces its ancestry back to these rulers, and also to a late fourteenth- or early fifteenth-century monarch known as the Cucumber King. The predecessor of the Cucumber King, so the story goes, was a man named Sihanu, himself inordinately fond of cucumbers. When he discovered the farmer who could grow the most succulent cucumbers in all of Cambodia, he made him his chamberlain, loaded him with honors, and told him to guard the royal cucumber patch with his life. Then, late one night, when the king was overcome by a craving for cucumbers and sneaked out to the patch for a snack, he was set upon and killed in the dark by his faithful guardian. Because they respected his fidelity, a council of elders voted the guardian king. He was the ancestor of Sihanouk.

Whether or not this story tells the tale of a long forgotten palace revolution, nobody knows. In any case, royal Cambodian genealogy is extremely complicated, with marriages between half brothers and sisters, and with the kings until recently blessed with many wives and concubines and shoals of princelings. The main thing is that Prince Sihanouk is descended from both Cambodian royal families, the Sisowaths and the Norodoms, who customarily took turns at the throne.

Recent Cambodian history is, if anything, even more difficult to describe in a paragraph than the golden past of Angkor. The last of Cambodia's absolute monarchs, Norodom Sihanouk, came to the throne eight months before Pearl Harbor. The Vichy French in 1941 relinquished control of Indochina to Japan, which awarded the two provinces of Battambang and Siemreap, the site of Angkor Vat, to Thailand as a supposedly faithful member of the Axis. It is said that the shock galvanized Cambodian intellectuals into action for the first time. After the war Cambodia got back her two lost provinces, and the last of Cambodia's absolute monarchs won a fight against the egalitarian Fourth Republic to translate his monarchy without delay into a constitutional one. After initial skirmishes with the Communist-supported Free Cambodia guerillas and other dissidents during a postwar period of turmoil (in 1953 a provincial governor was assassinated twenty miles outside Phnom-Penh), Sihanouk captured leadership of the independence movement, took the field himself against the Vietminh and the nationalists. He promised the rebel nationalists amnesty, and gradually brought them within the fold. His victory was sealed in 1954 with the Geneva Agreement which got the Vietminh forces out of his country within ninety days, and left Cambodia free to enter into foreign alliances and to accept economic and military aid at her own discretion.

The Americans and the Poles and the Russians and Chinese and French and others in Phnom-Penh to provide these things find themselves—usually for the first time—in a world of pagodas. Often, the walls of the pagodas are painted with crowds of demons and sea monsters, and the gold, flat-white and brick-red heroes of the *Ramayana,* with clashes between knobby-headed war elephants, and armies of bottle-green masked monkeys sailing through the air. Outside, in the courtyards of the pagodas, these same stories are danced by the young girls of the Royal Ballet, with the traditional golden-spired headdresses, whitened faces, and their golden shoulder boards swooping upwards like the pagodas' eaves, their long fingers curved backwards like those in the bas-reliefs at Angkor. They dance for the Cambodian Royal Family and its nobles, for officers of the United States Operations Mission, Chou En-lai and other notables: "The Battle between White Monkey and Black Monkey," "The Story of the Royal White Elephant," "Sita Abducted by Laksna" (danced in the forest), and "The Dance of the Fans."

Faubion Bowers has called the music of Cambodia—gongs, bells, bamboo xylophones, and ivory horns—the sound of clouds. I have also heard, within the precincts of the Royal Palace, somebody tootling "Alexander's Ragtime Band" on a clarinet. Almost anything can be found in the red and gold Royal Palace surveyed by neighboring tower whose four sides are faced with four pink-and-white lacquered masks. In the palace's Silver Pagoda the floor is indeed flagged with silver; there are Victorian crystal chandeliers, a silver Buddha and a jade Buddha and a great gold Buddha with pearls.

Among the royal treasures kept in a small building across the way are Cambodian coronation regalia: the fans, the ceremonial fly whisks, the four crowns worn by each monarch at various times during his accession—the first is a gold silk cap with ear flaps, ornamented with jewels and little flowers on long springs; the second is a crown designed to be worn in an automobile; the third is worn on horseback, and is a black suède cavalier's hat with a plumed golden band and a miniature crown fixed to the top; the fourth looks like a golden crash helmet with deep ear and neck flaps.

It all seems to fit in with the glassy, shining roofs of mustard or gold mosaic overhead, steep pitched, outlined in green and blue, with the ends of the dipping roofs curling outward and upward into space, half naga, half party tickler.

Dressed with Cambodian and French decorations gleaming

on their white tunics, worn with black shoes and long black stockings and the *sampots* hanging just below the knee like a wrap-around knicker of eggplant purple, dull gold, or metallic blue-green, the Khmer dignitaries alight from car or pedicab at the palace grounds for the Festival of the Dead or some other important traditional ceremony. One of the most impressive of all is ritual cremation. For the cremation of a great nobleman, a figure in the church, or a member of the Royal Family, a spired pavilion several stories high is built of bamboo and paper, yellow and cream and red and ochre and gold, and decorated with dark-green palm fronds and long white or red or yellow pennons flying from slender poles. The funeral cortège arrives with not-very-symmetrical rows of yellow-robed Buddhist priests chanting, with mourners in white, parasols and palanquins, musicians playing dirges on flute and drum, and sometimes soldiers and horses and elephants and a funeral car in the shape of a long golden dragon. At night, in the torchlight, there is the final conflagration.

The ashes and the bones of a king will be kept in a golden jar at the palace with those of his ancestors, and the ashes of his funeral pyre scattered on the Mekong. A year or more may go by between the death of a great man and his cremation; poor people may be obliged to bury their dead for a few years until enough money has been scraped together for exhumation, reverent washing and burning of the bones, and the placing of the ashes in a simple white earthenware pot to be cared for in perpetuity by the bonzes of the local pagoda.

The daily round in Phnom-Penh is tranquil enough, but there is an occasional flurry when one of the foreign missions calls in a "cultural" team to help woo the Cambodians. Most aspects of the Cold War have been studied and studied—

publications skirmishes, export and import offensives, competition in foreign aid—but there is a fine doctoral dissertation waiting for someone on the Communist-capitalist conflict by entertainment. This includes opera singers, violinists, ballet troupes, world's fairs, film festivals, puppet shows, circuses, soccer teams, weight lifters, ping-pong players, and masters of chess. In Cambodia the Khmer have been treated to barnstorming Soviet acrobats, Chinese folk dancers and plate twirlers, the singing and dancing Czechoslovak Ensemble Sluk, and from the United States, Benny Goodman (King Norodom Surmarit asked for "Blue Skies" and "Bugle Call Rag," and also made Mr. Goodman a Chevalier of the Order of Monisaraphon). Other Americans showing the flag have been two groups from *Le Far-Ouest: La Troupe G. Edward du Texas des États-Unis* featuring *Le Cow-Boy Américain* "in the flesh and bone," and a dancer named Tom Two Arrows (*Tom les Deux Flèches, Authentique Indien d'Amérique*). A US Air Force band has played town, and when they contributed to the Bonzes' Hospital in which they were put up overnight, they were all enrolled as Honorary Perpetual Members of the Society for Medical Assistance to Buddhist Priests.

As for the rest of the Cambodian Nights Entertainment, there is less of the French "cultural presence" than one would expect. The few French films which come to town compete with the Hollywood product, Indian films, or imports in Chinese from either Hong Kong or the Chinese mainland. The Chinese films run to Pekinese opera, full of war lords and emperors with long beards, celestial maidens and supernatural figures; or modern Chinese soap opera, with cuties in high collars and high-slit dresses. But nothing political—one Chinese propaganda film was banned shortly before the visit of

Chou En-lai. If I sound reserved about Chinese theater, perhaps I should add that a Chinese opera company, just across the street from the Hotel Lux where I stayed in Phnom-Penh, rattled, banged, crashed, and tinkled until one in the morning, and then there was an intermission for about three hours until the scullions began banging the crockery in tubs under my window.

About the only Gallic touch I could discern in the public entertainments of Phnom-Penh was the old French colonial habit of encouraging taxi dancing. There are usually a hundred or so taxi dancers in town, neat, very young Chinese, Vietnamese, and Cambodian girls who look like bright little butterflies, and who lead one another, holding hands, to the customers' tables. But the young intellectuals I met in Phnom-Penh knew the theater in Paris, had read Gide and Sartre as well as Racine and Molière, and talked enthusiastically about wedding the architecture of Le Corbusier and his disciples to that of the naga-enriched Khmer tradition. And the French have been infatuated with Cambodia since the Exposition Coloniale of 1908, when a Cambodian ballet troupe turned up, and Rodin wrote of the dancers: "They have found postures I had not dreamed of, movements which were unknown to us. . . ."

As against the few dozen Cambodians who speak fluent English and perhaps fifteen hundred who speak a little, there are a hundred thousand Cambodians who speak good French and another three hundred thousand—the school teachers and the civil servants in almost every village in the country—who speak a bit. The American Embassy has established a cultural beachhead with the translation of a number of American works including *Mutiny on the Bounty* and *Chicken Every Sunday,* and it sends about a dozen notable

Cambodians to the US each year (the bonzes go in their sandals and saffron robes, and this has worked out well enough except that one reported mildly that it was cold walking through the snow of Philadelphia).

Nobody knows exactly whether or not Cambodia is a member of the French Union. Prince Sihanouk has said that Cambodia cannot be a member of the French Union as it is now constituted. But if anything is changing, it is the French Union. And if Cambodia were to cut herself completely free from France, it is difficult to imagine the French legacy suddenly disappearing.

French economic aid to Cambodia (scholarships, forestry, an airport, a seaport) has cost the equivalent of better than twenty-five million dollars for each two-year period. Japanese aid is valued at a billion and a half yen over a three-year period. For the year 1958 alone, American military and economic aid amounted to forty million dollars' worth. This will pay for the army (the only neutral army I know of supported by Uncle Sam), equip the airport at Siemreap, and install a telegraphic network, as well as the possibility of long-term loans. Chinese aid to the tune of another 22½ million dollars' worth over two years will provide medicines for the Bonzes' Hospital built with American aid, and build a cement plant, paper and cloth mills, and a plywood factory.

India, Poland, and Czechoslovakia are all supplying electric plants and pumps, and Poland is furnishing an operating room in the hospital at Kompong Cham. India is sending agricultural and public health people as well as a professor of Sanskrit. As their first contribution, the Russians are building, staffing, and equipping a five-hundred-bed hospital in Phnom-Penh.

With the visiting chiefs of state bringing offers of aid,

Phnom-Penh has become almost as adept as New Delhi in welcoming distinguished visitors with arches of greenery and flags of two nations along the route of honor (New Delhi, which has evolved a welcome almost as standardized as New York's ticker tape parade, has turned out for both presidents of South Vietnam and North Vietnam within a few months of each other).

When the Prince visited the USSR, the Russians methodically strung up Cambodian-language banners saying "Long Live Sihanouk!" The first opposition team to reach Phnom-Penh was a rather old-fashioned band who ran to tunics, Bolshevik haircuts, and dour expressions—more nearly like a survival of the Leninist cloth cap days than the new urbanity—but they promised to help Cambodian industry, agriculture, and public health "without any selfish conditions, with full respect for the sovereignty and national dignity of Cambodia." Marshal Voroshilov of the Soviet Union had already presented Sihanouk with the Order of Suvarov First Class, and Sihanouk had presented Marshal Voroshilov with the Royal Order of Cambodia.

In the last of his four essays for *Réalités* on Communism in Cambodia, Norodom Sihanouk cut loose with about five thousand words which the paper ran under the banner headline:

N. SIHANOUK: "THE ANGLO-SAXONS ARE MAKING TWO ENEMIES OUT OF ONE IN CAMBODIA"

The piece by the Prince is rambling, but if I understand it, he says that the danger of Communist infiltration in Cambodia is surely there (he mentions as likely channels the many Cam-

bodian students in Paris and the Chinese and Vietnamese
minorities within the kingdom), that he himself is the only
barrier to the establishment of Communism in Cambodia,
but that this has been misunderstood by American diplomats
and by the American press which have given the impression
that his "neglect" and "complaisance" provide an opening to
the Communists in Cambodia which endangers the "so-called
Free World." On the contrary, says Sihanouk, by attacking
him as an inconstant saxophone-playing playboy blind to the
perils facing his people, his critics are playing into the hands
of the Communists. The flood of American anti-Communist
propaganda makes it difficult to control Communist anti-
American propaganda, accompanied by attempts at subver-
sion. Above all, American lack of understanding of the Asian
and Cambodian mind and character leads to a completely
contrary result than that which the United States hopes to
obtain through her aid to Cambodia, by far the most generous
given by any country. By complaining publicly that the
Cambodians are not grateful, by Congressional objections to
furnishing aid to a neutral nation, by rather obvious American
diplomatic attempts to influence Cambodian foreign policy,
by emphasizing that no one could prophesy if more aid would
be available for Cambodian projects the next year, Sihanouk
maintains that the American aid programs suffer by contrast
with those of the Russians and Chinese who simply announced
that they would contribute so much money to build a hospital
or a factory or whatever, attached no political conditions, and
made no promises or issued no warnings about future programs. "Sincerely," writes Sihanouk, "I believe that American
aid will never be fully appreciated by Asians until it appears
to be truly disinterested." Wagging an editorial finger, he

quotes the proverb: "The manner of giving is worth more than the gift."

Even while making allowances for this special Sihanoukian view of things, and for the political facts of life which so far have made it impossible for the President of the United States to extract from the American Congress anything more than short-term foreign aid a year at a time, it is interesting that many of Sihanouk's main points are those made by the most thoughtful critics and friends of foreign aid in the United States itself. Even his swipes in passing at America's support of strong men and police-state governments when they lend their support to American foreign policy and at American preference for military as opposed to economic aid have been made many, many times by thoughtful and responsible American observers—and were finding more and more of an editorial voice from the *Christian Science Monitor* to the New York *Herald Tribune*. In some respects American public opinion has been moving more quickly than Congress, especially toward acceptance of foreign aid for neutrals, and emphasis on economic rather than military aid: in early 1957 the New York *Times* reported that a continuing study by the University of Chicago on behalf of the US Government showed 52 per cent of the people polled were "in favor of economic aid to neutral nations like India (against 43 per cent less than a year before), 80 per cent in favor of "technical assistance to under-developed nations," and found that 71 per cent of them thought "economic aid to friendly nations more important than military aid" (only 51 per cent believed so six years before).

Actually, after a few false starts and a period of trial and error, the American economic missioners have worked out a program which looks very good: beginning with a photo-offset printing plant presented to the Cambodian government, the program has proliferated until it embraces the teaching of teachers, foresters, firemen, doctors, nurses and midwives, health and sanitation, communications, forestry, agriculture and livestock. The prides of the project are the Bonzes' Hospital; the hundred-and-thirty-mile, fifteen-million-dollar road running from the capital down to the new port which the French have built at Kompong Som, larger than those of either Saigon or Bangkok, and freeing Cambodia from dependence on her two neighbors who, until the intervention of the French, had whittled Cambodia's frontiers down to a point where the kingdom was almost ready to disappear; and the rehabilitation of the eleventh-century classical Khmer irrigation system around Angkor Vat.

There was at first little visible co-ordination of Cambodian aid by her benefactors, Eastern or Western, and not much more by the object of their affections. The Khmer government asked donors, as they presented themselves, for bits and pieces she felt she needed, and there have been charges that she sometimes asked two prospects for funds for the same program at the same time.

The Royal School of Medicine, built jointly with Cambodian and American funds and staffed with French professors, was a later and happier example, and much needed (its first full-fledged doctors, graduating in 1960, will join the half-dozen existing Cambodian doctors, including a Paris-trained psychiatrist). The brick-red American highway that runs down to the French port at Kompong Som is another example, and so is French and American aid to rural co-ops to encourage loans at low rates of interest in the hope of delivering the Cambodian farmer from that traditional scourge, the moneylender. There are allied French efforts with twenty-five agricultural men in the field.

The annual American bill equals about three quarters of the Cambodian budget, split roughly between military and economic aid, with the United States paying an annual eighteen million dollars for the Cambodian Army of thirty thousand men, the same size as the Lao Army. It is difficult to imagine an economy-minded American Congress coming across with much more—jets, for instance, as in Thailand—unless Communist troops were breathing down the Cambodians' necks, in which case it might well be too late.

In the flurry of foreign aid, it is fair to remember that the now celebrated Communist offensive, complete with assistance to underdeveloped countries, seems to have been inspired by the American effort, and the success of the Marshall Plan in Europe.

In the international aid handicap, a favorite advertisement is now "No Strings Attached," a phrase in English which has been seized upon with great enthusiasm by the Russians and Chinese and their client countries. It is often enough echoed by the recipients, though I have never been quite sure whether the latter completely believe this, or whether by repetition they hope to make it come true. A newer Chinese Communist stock phrase, "Great Nation Chauvinism," recurs in the Peking litanies as one of the things they've sworn off. Originally a description of the dominant Han Chinese rather sniffy attitude toward their own non-Han national minorities, the phrase has been turned around for use on the major Western powers, and was picked up and used in just that sense by Sihanouk in his newspaper series.

I went to call on the Chinese economic mission not long after its arrival from Peking. By that time I had moved to the

Hôtel le Royal, and I met them first at the desk where I was trying to collect my mail, and they kept getting in the way of its delivery by negotiating with the management a crash job of catering for a party they wanted to give that same day, in honor of Chinese aid, for "Tout Phnom-Penh," Americans excepted. The hosts asked that no American drinks be served; scotch, they said, would be all right. After a couple of days, when things had quieted down, I called on Mr. Yeh Ching-hao, Head of the Economic Mission of the People's Republic of China, and Mr. Tsao Kuei-sheng, his Deputy. I hope I am not guilty of Great Nation Chauvinism when I say that the hour and a half I spent with them was easily the most uninformative hour and a half I have ever spent with any spokesman for anything anywhere. Mr. Yeh and his colleagues spoke English with American accents and they wore batteries of fountain pens clipped to their breast pockets, but they were politely vague as to whether the billion dollars of Chinese aid offered to Egypt, North Korea, North Vietnam, Nepal, Cambodia, and Laos marked the beginning of a Peking program for economic assistance throughout Asia and the Middle East. "You can have all the informations in the newspapers," said Mr. Yeh, evenly.

On his famous whirlwind tour through south Asia and on to Moscow, Warsaw, and Budapest, the Chinese Premier, Chou En-lai, spent just under a week in Phnom-Penh, only a few days less than he did in India. The customary joint communiqué signed by Sihanouk and Chou called for Chinese-Cambodian relations which would be a "model of international coöperation," and some of the foreign correspondents trying to keep up with Mr. Chou on his gallopade, and who had known him well enough in the old days in China, believed that he may have meant just that. If the neighbors can be persuaded that Cambodia has managed to accept a 22½-million-dollar gift from the Chinese dragon with no more perilous outcome than a blizzard of paper announcing the outbreak of love and fraternity between the two nations, or possibly the expense of exchanging dance troupes, then the neighbors may be emboldened to try it too. China's gain is clear: just as she is able to still the fears of the smaller nations around her, so the anti-Communist front loses strength. If Mr. Chou and his government can convince the Cambodians that China will practice, and not just preach, the principles of co-existence, that she really wants to help the Cambodians and not just gobble them up, then China will have taken another long step along what foreign observers see as the land route to the tin, rubber, and rice of Malaya, Indonesia, and Thailand.

The test will be the behavior of the quarter of a million Chinese in Cambodia, the essentially apolitical, industrious minority which controls the commerce of the country. Mr. Chou has told his kinsmen to be good Cambodian citizens. It would be a sophisticated gamble, and one which might pay off all the way across Asia in the long run. But after Prince Sihanouk's visit to Peking, the proportion of Chinese Cambodian schools using Communist textbooks jumped from about a third to three-quarters; two Chinese newspapers embraced Communism and two new Chinese Communist papers began publication, leaving only one Chinese newspaper in Cambodia which is non-Communist. There were, when I visited Phnom-Penh, correspondents for the Peking *People's Daily* and the New China News Agency, from Tass and the (North) Vietnamese News Agency. From time to time the ubiquitous Wilfred Burchett turns up, representing the London *Daily Worker*, Paris *Humanité*, Moscow *New Times*, and Delhi's Communist party weekly *New Age*, as well as Radio

Peking and Radio Hanoi. Mrs. Burchett, Mme Burchett Ossi-kova, represented the Bulgarian Press. The Western world was normally represented only by staff men from Agence France-Presse, Reuter, and AP, with occasional visits from correspondents on tour.

As much as it can lie in the hands of any one man, the future of Cambodia is in the hands of Norodom Sihanouk. So I went to call on the Prince, and he was good enough to receive me one day just after he had completed his weekly reception of anyone who wanted to see him—widows, disgruntled office-holders, peasants with a village quarrel, litigants who felt they could not find justice in the courts. We sat there in a drawing room of his palace, on a couch shaped like a half moon and covered with egg-yellow silk, sipping the glasses of cham-pagne which seem indispensable to Gallic protocol, even in the morning.

There was a circular rug of royal blue on the floor, more chairs covered with the same yellow silk, and bright splashes of tropical flowers in silver bowls, canary with crimson, vivid pink against apple green. The drawing room was light and airy, with overhead fans, and on the walls were olive-green bas-reliefs of the classical Khmer dancing girls from Angkor Vat. Outside were the naga balustrades, and overhead, the swooping, telescopic roofs and the many-tiered towers shining in the sun.

The Prince of Cambodia has been described in terms guar-anteed to excite anyone's curiosity. He seems to fascinate even his detractors, who spent a remarkable amount of time ex-plaining his unimportance. Diplomats and professional politi-cal observers often find him hard to classify; within forty-eight hours after John Foster Dulles left him in Phnom-Penh, thinking all was relatively serene, he was handed the news that Sihanouk had abdicated and was off on a new tack. A French friend who has worked with the Prince from time to time says of Sihanouk: "He is a fish, he is an eel. You will never catch him. This flirt with the Communists. He promises them the moon, and gives them a grain of sand.

"He is a wonderful subject for a dramatist," said my French friend. "He has something of the temperament of a musician. Just when you think you can no longer count on him, then he gives you his shirt. At a press conference he will say, 'Excuse me, I am not too brilliant—I haven't slept for thirty-eight hours.' And in the provinces, Sihanouk is still king."

According to one report, Cambodians say they can see Norodom Sihanouk's face in the moon.

The Prince who has so captured the imagination and the interest of his friends and enemies was wearing the day I met him a dove-gray linen suit, shiny black shoes with black suède panels, a white figured shirt with a soft collar and oblong gold cuff-links. On his left wrist was a Lao *bassi* bracelet of cotton threads. There were a few white hairs in the squarish black pompadour that framed his face, plump, but not nearly so chubby as in his photographs. His voice was high-pitched, his gestures quick, fluid, intense, and sometimes theatrical, and he looked young enough to be an undergraduate.

"What I want is a democracy and a constitutional monarchy. And a little social progress. When I am absent for three months, there is anarchy. People say that I vaunt myself when I say that I fight alone. I don't. I wish there were lots of people to help me fight. But there aren't, I have tried and tried. I am alone." The Prince sounded plaintive.

"Since the conference at Bandung," said the Prince, after a pause, "the African and Asian nations have had a single aim—independence from foreign domination. Allen Dulles of your

Central Intelligence Agency missed the depth of this feeling when he said to me that North Vietnam is, after all, completely under the thumb of China. The thing that counted among the Vietnamese people was that Ho fought the French for independence.

"We have been deeply touched by aid from India and Pakistan and Ceylon under the Colombo Plan," said the Prince, "but we have not yet consolidated Asian economic cooperation and cultural exchange. Each Asian nation," said the Prince, speaking carefully and using an adjective that surprised me, "still turns to the white nations, to the United States and Russia."

The Prince spoke quickly, in extremely good French, sometimes with a dash of university slang, often ironically or extravagantly, sometimes for effect, sometimes just for the fun of it. But it is clear that—if he is thespian and quicksilver, and if he sometimes permits himself unstatesmanlike jokes or emotional outbursts in public—he is obviously capable and determined, and has an imagination and inventiveness not too common among monarchs. He appeared very far from the figure of fun or the one-man government-by-huff he has seemed to some.

"I am not a pessimist," said the Prince, "but I am a stubborn man. I shall be strict. I have forced the rich functionaries to return the cars and houses they have taken." He sighed. "But I haven't really triumphed yet. I can't even get people to pay taxes. Not the new taxes. The *old* taxes."

At home and abroad Sihanouk continues his journey across the high wire. As the princely preceptor of a newly independent, not-very-large and not-very-powerful kingdom, he has multiplied the strength of his country severalfold. Though brought up as a princeling in an absolute monarchy of an

Oriental splendor that verged on that of the Ballet Russe of Diaghilev and Bakst, Norodom Sihanouk has grasped the point that his own people as well as other Africans and Asians will not much longer tolerate with the old submissiveness the idea of political dependence as ordained by the gods and the nobility.

"There are theoretically several ways this country could fall to the Communists," said a Canadian friend then living in Phnom-Penh. "Force, pressure just short of force, or peaceful penetration. And there is one other possibility—that the powers, including the Communists, think it to their best interest to keep Cambodia neutral. You Americans seem to think Sihanouk is a barefoot boy just in from the country. You think the Communists are bound to take him. But I'm not so sure, I'm not so sure. . . ."

14 MONSIEUR MARCHAL AND ANGKOR VAT

ONE day after a couple of months in Vientiane, I saw striding along the road into town a slight, smallish gentleman with bright blue eyes, white hair, and a white goatee, not only agile but cricketlike in his movements. He kept turning up in front of pagodas, and on the famous two-lane asphalt highway that led from Vientiane several miles along the way to the great sixteenth-century walled stupa called Tat Luang. He was Henri Marchal, Honorary Chief of the École Française d'Extrême-Orient's Archeological Service and long director of the restorations at Angkor Vat, now emerged from retirement for the second or third time, on loan to the government of Laos to restore their pagodas and religious monuments. Sometimes he was to be found in a pedicab, but more often he was on foot, marching along with a squarish, woven Buddhist carry-all looped over one arm.

He lived in the École Française villa on a shady knoll off the road between an exuberant shack of a roadhouse and the vague pastureland around the Palais du Gouvernement, sharing a roomy house and its EFEO library with the anthropologist Lafont and his wife. When I got to know them better, I spent an evening with M. Marchal looking at his stereoptican views, over the years of archeological exploration in India, Ceylon, Java, China, and above all, Cambodia, where he became curator of Angkor in 1908, less than four years after he'd stepped off the boat in Indochina, a young architect fresh out of the Beaux-Arts.

"When I arrived half a century ago," said M. Marchal, "all the Chinese wore pigtails. A few years later came the Chinese Revolution, and they cut them all off." He showed us a sepia view of Kunming, the capital of Yunnan, at the end of the Burma Road and the railway from Vietnam. There were more pictures of the layered architecture of northern India, of the Ganges with corpses by the burning ghats. A photograph of the cremation of the Cambodian King Norodom in 1906 showed a part of his harem of five hundred, dressed in white robes of mourning, heads shaven, seated before the pyre. It was odd to reflect that Norodom had come to the throne a century ago, and that our host had lived in Norodom's kingdom during the reign of that king.

Henri Marchal's family had stayed behind in Siemreap among the temples to whose restoration he had given most of his life. He planned to retire for the last time, "definitively" as he kept saying, before too many months or years were out, but in the meantime, he said, he would be happy to take a couple of weeks' holiday and visit his family. He said modestly that he would show me his work. It was like having a pharaoh ask one to inspect his pyramid. We made the trip together, and I'm not sure which impressed me more, Angkor Vat or its *Ancien Conservateur*.

On the early morning plane on the way down, I asked a lot of questions, trying to learn what had brought Henri Marchal to Indochina. "I was born in front of the Gare Montparnasse on the twenty-fourth of June in 1876," said M. Marchal. "My mother's family were Old Paris, but my father's family came from Lorraine. He was an engineer in a fire pump plant, and my grandfather was a jeweler. I'm the Lorraine type."

M. Marchal's eyes were undoubtedly blue, but beyond that, I couldn't be sure what the Lorraine type was. He was perhaps five feet five, but bowed. His white hair was short-cropped and his skin pink, with a fine crisscross of wrinkles, and strong lines across his forehead. He wore a short-sleeved shirt with an open collar, a pair of old washable trousers, and rubber sandals, and he carried a pair of steel-rimmed spectacles which he put on occasionally to read fine print. I remembered that a few times he wore a jacket in Indochina he had in his buttonhole the ribbon of the Chevalier and the rosette of the Officer of the Legion of Honor.

"I went to school in Paris at seven," said M. Marchal. "I remember we had Egyptian history at fourteen. I took my *bachot* at seventeen, a pre-architectural course for two years, and at nineteen, went to the Beaux-Arts for four years. I became a domestic architect, and in 1905 went to Cambodia to join the Public Works Department in Battambang, building houses. In 1908 I went to Angkor as a tourist. Then from 1916 through 1937 I was there as director, the second. My predecessor was assassinated by pirates in a payroll robbery in the jungle. My successor committed suicide with a revolver I loaned him for protection. All together, I spent twenty-seven years at Angkor, and the other seven curators less than two years each." M. Marchal seemed happy that he had been allowed to spend so much time there.

When we came down at Siemreap, I checked in at the local hotel, and M. Marchal went off to his house on Boulevard Henri Marchal, where I went to call on him and meet his family. On one side of the road the little Siemreap River meandered like a brook. On the other was a red, green, and white signboard giving the street number in Cambodian, and sitting on it, a large buff-and-red agama lizard. From the road a dirt track led a few yards to the house, set in a grove of coconut palms, papayas, bananas, and grapefruit trees. It was a well-made Cambodian village house, on stilts, and very much like the ones in Laos. On the steps and the veranda were playing two small girls, M. Marchal's descendents, a towhead with blue eyes and her cousin who looked like a brown Cambodian sprite with bangs.

With some difficulty I began to sort out M. Marchal's family. In 1904, he and Marie-Gerny were married in France, and she followed him to Indochina two years later, helping him with his work. Their granddaughter is married to a young Cambodian architect. They already have children of their own, Henri Marchal's great-grandchildren.

M. Marchal's French wife died. His second wife is Cambodian, a solid, smiling woman who wears a sarong and the Cambodian older women's crew cut. Their Franco-Khmer daughter married a French engineer. The children seem to take the best from both worlds. It is a very nice international salad.

M. Marchal looked over his family, sitting on the ladder-like front steps as I took their picture, and said cheerfully, "When I am here definitively, I shall have goat's milk delivered every day."

M. Marchal borrowed a jeep, and we set off for Angkor Vat, one of perhaps a thousand great monuments, temples, and cities scattered over the peninsula. Some sixty have been gradually detached from the jungle around Siemreap. Angkor Vat is by no means the largest. Nor is it the most beautiful. Many have at least one other candidate for the most awesome. But Angkor Vat is by long odds the most celebrated. It has been described by everybody from Pierre Loti to the *National Geographic*. Its towers are on the national flag and on Cambodian currency, on postage stamps and tourist folders, and on the shoulder patches of the twenty-nine officers and thirty enlisted men of the U.S. military aid mission in Cambodia. Everyone is taken to Angkor. Chou En-lai made the guided tour, and declared himself suitably impressed. I am only sorry that Mark Twain, who was as near as India, didn't find his way.

Because its proportions are nearly perfect, Angkor Vat seen from the air is tidy and not especially overwhelming: a steep series of platforms with four towers like sculptured pine cones frame a fifth and larger tower at their center. The high central platform falls away to a courtyard surrounded by a gallery, and this is framed by a strip of grass and another, outer gallery. The whole is enclosed by a rectangular moat. But from the tables of the open-air café opposite the temple's entrance, across the road built by the Travaux Publiques, the causeway which leads across the water-and-lotus mirrors to the towers of Angkor Vat is a good quarter of a mile long. And the moat reflecting the clouds and towers stretches some two and a half miles. Night comes quickly here, and even by moonlight it is difficult to make out the steps and cubes and masses of the fortresslike temple, with the greater masses looming behind. After dark the faint orange spots of the neighbors' cigarettes glow as they sit by the moat, and sometimes someone plays the accordion or mandolin. The bonzes chant evening prayers at the monastery to the left inside the outer stone portal, and small boys with resin torches scout for tourists at the entrance. Inside, the bats chitter by the hundreds in the vaulted roofs, the statue of Vishnu dances in the torchlight, and the reliefs of old gods and battles, and the infinity of sculptures of the Buddha recede quickly into the darkness of the corridors. It is a handsome and a spooky place.

In the daytime twilight of the galleries, the gray limestone bas-reliefs stretch for several miles along the walls. They look like tapestries. Here is King Suryavarman II who built the temple as his tomb, and in honor of Shiva and Vishnu, whom, as the guidebook says, he would join after his death. He looks elegant and composed as he sits on a low table ornamented with nagas, surrounded with ceremonial fans and fly whisks, and sheltered by a cloudbank of flat ceremonial parasols like pie tins upside down. There are a good eight thousand other figures: chariots and archers and armies and slaves and gods riding on peacocks and kings on elephants. The facilities of the temple include monumental doorways so that guests of mark may enter on their elephants. "I used elephants myself at the debut," said M. Marchal. "In 1920 it was far easier to reach Bantei Srei and the outlying temples by elephant. I like them very much for long trips. They don't need a road, they go right through the forest. Much better than a horse. But unfortunately, in 1940 they were stolen."

Even more fetching than the elephants are the *apsaras* and *tevodas,* carved in relief along the walls, the heavenly dancers and courtesans whose jewelry and coiffures are much the same as those of the present Royal Ballet, but who were considerably less covered. The fingers of the dancers are bent backward as they are today. They have narrow waists with ripe breasts and bellies after the Indian ideal, but with a half smile that is Cambodian, and their lips and breasts have smooth highlights polished by the fingertips of curious and pious pilgrims.

As you move inward through the long, dim galleries a little light comes from the mullioned windows, their bars worked like balustrades turned on a lathe. The Hindu deities and the later Buddhas sitting peacefully in the gloom shine with subtle traces of red and gold where the faithful have stuck gold leaf on wet red lacquer. The steps mount as one walks toward the center of the temple city, for the galleries are rectangles within rectangles, like a nest of boxes, until at the center the steps rise almost vertically to a platform nearly two hundred feet above the ground of the surrounding meadows. Here, outside the central shrine and the five towers of the quincunx, it is rather like looking down from the trestle toward the take-off of a ski jump; tourists sometimes freeze at the top and have to be helped down by two men, one at each leg.

We sat on the steps in the early morning sun, and M. Marchal talked of the building of Angkor and the other temples. "The Khmer were fine sculptors. They had a genius for the monumental. But from the purely architectural point of view, they were terrible," said the man who above all else loved the architecture of Angkor. He admired their spaciousness, their sense of proportion, but was not prepared to admit that they knew how to put stones together. The blocks in many of the temples were roughly fitted without mortar, and by no means with the precision of the Incas of Peru. Often enough, the sculpture begun at the bottom of a frieze continued bravely upward for a bit, and then petered out toward the top. Those at Angkor Vat were joined by a film of glue. Of its composition no one is sure; the architectural critic

Michael Sullivan has suggested that it may be the old Thai formula of honey, hair, and boiled cowhide.

When all allowances have been made for rough finishing, for a certain heaviness and repetition, the temples of Angkor remain one of the most extraordinary things on the face of this earth. The massive walls and stairs and towers rising out of the jungle are not graceful or, to me, beautiful. Rather they are overwhelming, and in a way, a little menacing. The system of moats and causeways, roads and lakes which are great reflecting basins has something of the frozen formality of Versailles. But Osbert Sitwell, who is not easily bowled over, has written plainly: "Let it be said immediately that Angkor, as it stands, is the chief wonder of the world today, one of the summits to which human genius has aspired in stone, infinitely more impressive, lovely, and, as well, romantic than anything that can be seen in China. . . ."

When Henri Mouhot, the French botanist who in 1860 rediscovered Angkor, asked the latter-day Khmer living around the ruins who had built these colossal monuments, "they invariably made one or other of these four answers: 'It is the work of the King of Angels, my Lord,' 'It is the work of giants,' 'We owe these buildings to the Leper King,' or, finally, 'They built themselves.'"

There had been a population of some two million living in the villages whose offerings supported the temples in the region of Angkor, said M. Marchal as we sat on the ancient steps, talking of this and that. The inscribed hospital stelae of King Jayavarman VII, the late twelfth-century builder of the walls of Angkor Thom and its Bayon, found as far away as the province of Vientiane, commemorate the 102 infirmaries spread across the Khmer Empire at the time of its greatest extent, each open to all castes, and with 101 attendants, including two sacrificers and one astronomer. The country was rich, and there were slaves from Burma and Thailand and from the rival Kingdom of Champa in what is now central Vietnam. Great numbers of slaves were needed to keep pace with the frenzied building of funerary piles and temples to the deities and themselves by the Khmer god-emperors. A rich household might keep a hundred slaves, a middle-class household ten to twenty, and only the poorest of the poor among the Khmer, no slaves at all.

Fa Ngoum, the ancestor of the present Lao dynasty and the founder of the original Lao kingdom of Lan Xan, came to Angkor as a child about 1320 with his rebellious father, fleeing his grandfather who was king of that northern royal capital which became Luangprabang. At the court of Angkor, Fa Ngoum was brought up by a Buddhist monk, and at sixteen, he married a daughter of the Khmer king. About 1350 he and his father were given a Khmer army of ten thousand to attempt to take his grandfather's throne. Three years later, his father was dead, his grandfather conquered, and Fa Ngoum the first king of the united Land of the Million Elephants and the White Parasol.

But 1350 was also the year the people of Ayudhya, the old Mon and Thai capital just north of Bangkok, began to attack the Khmer with increasing ferocity. The Khmer were rich, strong, and vigorous, and these were the days of Angkor's greatest glory. But it was the beginning of the end, and by 1430 the armies of Ayudhya—which itself now lies in ruins—captured and sacked Angkor.

That was a year before Joan of Arc was burned at the stake in France. When Fa Ngoum reached Angkor, Dante was completing his *Divine Comedy*. Marco Polo had lately returned to Italy from China. In a few years the Black Death would kill about a quarter of the people in Europe. The pharaohs who built the pyramids had disappeared a millennia ago, and Rome had fallen to the barbarians some nine hundred years before. But Leif Ericson had only sighted "Vinland," if that was North America, a couple of hundred years earlier. The Second Maya Empire still flourished in Yucatan, and that of the Incas in the high Andes. But because of the visit of a member of one of the sporadic Chinese missions which arrived to report on the Southern Barbarians, and to extract tribute if possible—Chou Ta-kuan, who visited Angkor in 1296 and 1297—there exists a clearer, more vivid picture of daily life in the capital of the ancient Khmer Empire than there does of the great Amerindian civilizations, or of Egypt, or, in the opinion of Sitwell, of classical Rome.

Kublai Khan had been unsuccessful in persuading the Khmer to submit to the Mongol court at Peking, and so after his death in 1294, his successor Timur Khan sent another embassy which reached Angkor at the end of the reign of Jayavarman VIII, and spent more than a year there in another attempt to extract tribute. Chou Ta-kuan appears to have accompanied this embassy as a sort of commercial attaché. He says that the Khmer duly rendered homage, but no trace of any subsequent payment has been found.

The report of Chou Ta-kuan is that of a highly intelligent, trained observer whose simple style, curiosity, and humor remind me a little of an Eastern version of Charles Darwin putting ashore from H.M.S. *Beagle* at Tierra del Fuego or one of the more improbable South American ports. Chou's description of life in Angkor was discovered in the Imperial Archives in Peking, and translated and published in 1902 by Paul Pelliot of the École Française d'Extrême-Orient.

Osbert Sitwell in his wonderfully evocative Oriental sketch

book *Escape with Me!* has translated the remarkable account of Chou Ta-kuan from the French:

The King puts on a diadem of gold, or, if he omits to do this, twists around his chignon a garland of sweet-smelling flowers, a kind of jasmine. Round his neck he carries a heavy necklace of large pearls, and on his wrists and ankles and fingers are bracelets and rings of gold, in which are set "cats'-eyes." He goes about unshod, but the soles of his feet as well as his palms are rouged. He holds a sword of gold in his hand when he leaves the Palace. . . .

. . . Cavalry always head the escort, then follow the standards, the pennants and the music, and, in their rear, between three and five hundred Girls of the Palace, in flowered dresses and with blossoms in their hair, holding in their hands huge wax candles, which are alight even in the day-time. More Girls of the Palace now bear the royal vessels of gold and silver. Behind marches another company of Girls of the Palace, carrying lances and shields; Amazons, these constitute the private bodyguard of the King. After them, come carriages drawn by goats, and carriages drawn by horses, all ornamented with gold. The ministers and princes are mounted on elephants, and going in front, scan the distance; their red parasols are not to be counted for number. Next, the wives and the concubines of the King drive by, in palanquins and howdahs (they have certainly more than a hundred parasols embellished with gold): and behind them, erect on the back of an elephant—its tusks encased in gold—stands the King, holding in his hand the precious sword. Twenty white parasols surround the presence, and a squadron of cavalry for protection. Those who see the King are supposed to prostrate themselves and touch the ground with their foreheads: if they fail to do this, they are seized by the Masters of Ceremonies, who do not release them without their paying for it.

It is this sword which a good many people believe is the same golden sword still among the imperial regalia at the palace in Phnom-Penh. Certainly the Khmer who live in Phnom-Penh or Siemreap are very much like those surviving on the bas-reliefs. At Angkor Thom, the temple city near Angkor Vat, whose precincts are several times its size, hundreds of the thousands of flat, busy figures which crowd its friezes wear the same chignon once worn by the Khmer Emperor and which are still the mode among the women of Laos; they use the same oxcarts, drive the same elephants, live in houses with the same steep, swooping, hooked roofs, use the same knives and other tools and hunt with the same crossbows used by the contemporary Khmer who live about the ruins, and on occasion materialize out of the woods bearing the crossbows to sell to tourists.

The officers in the carvings are larger than the mercenaries and the slaves they capture, and the kings seem giants with their doll-sized wives. Warriors wear tunics of small square or diamond pattern, and minimal breech-clouts. In their off moments they go to cockfights, as their descendents seven hundred years later still do. Between split sticks they cook the same fish that still feed Cambodia's semiaquatic population. When the Khmer are fighting the Chams in bas-relief, the ships colliding in combat carry crude anchors like those used by Chinese junks of our own century, and their prows look suspiciously like contemporary nagas. Fallen warriors mingle with great fish in the water, and some are being chewed by what appear to be stuffed crocodiles.

Just to the north of Angkor Vat, I climbed with M. Marchal through the Bayon at the center of Angkor Thom, each of whose earthen city walls stretches for nearly seven miles and a half, through the broken columns and the weathered

stone, through the deep, dark labyrinthine reliefs of Jayavarman VII's battles with the Chams, up the interminable
steps of stone to the rudely pyramidal towers, whose four
sides each bear a mask, larger than a man, of the king,
splotched with lichens, brooding, smiling faintly, looking out
over the four corners of his kingdom. Similar towers are
thought to have watched over the farthest corners of his
realm, up to Chieng Mai in what is now northeast Thailand
but used to be Laos. These extraordinary faces are a favorite with artists and post-card manufacturers. They are known
nowhere else but here at Angkor Thom, where there are sixteen of them, colossal, smiling and sleepless, looking out from
the central heights of the Bayon, a dozen more at the end of
each of its cruciform approaches, and more giant, enigmatic
faces over the monumental gateways at each of the city's
cardinal points. It is a strange and disturbing motif, difficult
to forget by moonlight.

"When I first came here in 1908," said M. Marchal, as
we rested, "this was jungle. Angkor Vat was more or
less protected because there is a bonzerie next door, and
the bonzes took care of the buildings. But in Angkor Thom,
the forest was everywhere. Even the columns were being
eaten by the trees." He explained the process of anastylosis
by which he had reconstructed Angkor Thom and the other
monuments, stone by stone, first pulling them all down, and
then replacing them in the proper order, after pouring a
concrete foundation.

M. Marchal began to reminisce about the first days of the
French at Angkor. When he first saw it, it belonged to Thailand, which then called itself Siam, and the old Siamese flag
with its fat white elephant in profile, protected the ruins.
His eyes, sometimes bright blue, sometimes bluish-gray, lit

up, and his arms waved in Gallic gestures. We were talking about a famous Buddha we had seen together in Bangkok: "But that Buddha has absolutely *no* artistic value," he said with passion, yet with no unkindness. When he stood up, he had a little potbelly, and he leaned backward from the waist, though his white head thrust foreward in a scholar's stoop. I thought of his comment in his handsome album *Les Temples d'Angkor:* "the damned are thin and the large stomach is reserved for the chosen and for the gods." (Of all the books on Angkor, this one of Henri Marchal strikes me as the most deeply informative, the most gracefully written, and the best.)

On the walls around us, the ranks of flat and chubby stone citizens of Angkor went about their business: building ships, preparing for childbirth, selling things at the market, searching for lice in one another's hair, on pilgrimage to hermits and holy places, eating pork and *pâtés,* going off to war with gongs beating and a buffoon in attendance. These are the same market women and artisans of whom Chou Ha-kuan wrote, when the jungle paths and the new roads of the Travaux Publiques were imperial highways busy with elephants and parasols and people. The King, wrote Chou Ta-kuan, held two public audiences daily, when at the sound of conch horns, two or three Girls of the Palace "raise the curtain with their little fingers," and the King appears at the window holding his golden sword. From China, Chou Ta-kuan reported, the Cambodians imported blue porcelain, lacquer trays, mercury and vermilion, pewter, paper, sulphur, saltpeter, sandalwood, orrisroot, wooden combs, needles, copper utensils and iron pots, mats, musk, canvas, oils, targets, and parasols of red taffeta and umbrellas of green oiled silk with a short fringe. In return, the Cambodians exported to China the wings of

kingfishers, iridescent blue and green, to be made into brides'
tiaras.

"The women, for their part, are most lascivious, so people
say," wrote the Chinese visitor, and as he went on to describe
the customs of the country, he became more and more dis-
mayed. "Thus if a husband finds himself called away on business to distant parts for any length of time, all will be well
for a few nights. But after ten or so have passed, his wife
will not fail to make the complaint: 'I am not a spirit. Why
should I sleep alone?' Even to such lengths does their de-
pravity extend!" Chou Ta-kuan recorded that male homosexu-
als in groups of ten or more lurked in the public square, and
tried to entice the Chinese who they hoped would give them
presents ("It is hideous, it is shocking!").

"Then the people of this country are very often ill, largely
due to their too frequent baths and washings of the head.
They seem particularly liable to leprosy (there was even a
'Leper King,' but nobody thought the worse of him for it!).
But, in the humble opinion of this writer, it is their amatory
excesses, together with over-indulgence in baths (scarcely
have they finished one thing, than they begin the other, so
it is said). Everyone here washes far too much: the country
is so hot that one cannot get through the day without several
baths, and even in the night, one feels obliged to get up and
have another bath or two. . . ."

Chou Ta-kuan reported that the Cambodian medicines
differed from the Chinese, and that there were witch doctors
("Ludicrous!"). He told how pious parents of little girls between the ages of ten and eleven had them ceremonially de-
flowered by bonzes rewarded for this service with wine, rice,
areca nuts, silk, and silver plate, with a great banquet and
a parade with palanquins and musicians—so popular a cere-

mony that there might be as many as ten going on at once in a single street ("Appalling din!").

At Phra Khan, a temple named after the King's sacred sword, as we made our way around, it was slippery and wet, with a misty rain falling, and the sky a great *gouache* of gray and off-white. From out of the forest of pinkish and oyster-splotched trees, shy brown children peeked through the doorways while M. Marchal explained the reconstruction going on there in the wet. Through a series of doors and openings like perspective in a toy theater, we could see the workmen, in shorts and sometimes with handkerchiefs tied round their heads, wrestling with the tremendous slabs of fallen stone, working a derrick improvised from a tripod, a block and tackle and a long chain which they pulled swiftly hand over hand to hoist the blocks ever so slowly so that they could be carried away by the little carts that trundled into the dripping forest on the miniature railroad. The ruined walls all around being numbered and dismantled were bumpy and chipped undressed stone, for they were never finished— the builders inexplicably left in a hurry. The stone was like the lees of old wine, a smoky dark red and gray and a blackish- reddish-brown, with cobwebs in the doorways of the little inner temples, and lichens growing a beautiful buff and bot- tle green and dark emerald. In one of the broken shrines where we took shelter from the rain, there was the odor of bats in the air, the light bisque statue of Vishnu was richly dressed in pea-green mold, but his face was smiling and serene. Some of the statues were enriched with many of the little figures called Bhodisatvas, sort of apprentice Buddhas in an earlier stage of their journey toward perfection—and because not so perfect, often more popular with the faithful.

At Phra Khan and the other temples where work was in progress, M. Marchal explained that the seemingly makeshift bamboo scaffolding that ran erratically up the sides of the stonework (as it climbs twelve-story buildings in Hong Kong) was pliant and strong and far more efficient than metal, which expands in the sun and comes in specified lengths. And over the days, as we clambered up and down the monuments, I learned something of what had brought him to Indochina.

"My mother and father told me stories about the Franco-Prussian War," he said one day as we were talking about Paris Voisin's wartime zoölogical menu. "I know they ate rats, but I am not sure about animals in the zoo . . . Dreyfus was a soldier in my regiment. . . .

"When I was a student, I went a lot to the *Opéra* and to the *Opéra Comique*. I used to go to the *Comédie Française* to see *Cyrano* and Racine and Molière and Corneille. I often went to see Henrik Ibsen—*Maison de la Poupée, Peer Gynt, Enmi du Peuple, Henri Bataille*. I read de Maupassant and Alphonse Daudet and Anatole France. In all my youth, I was always taken up with the arts—by painting and sculpture, theater, music, literature, dance—never by science.

"Of the painters I liked Gustave Moreau, Manet, and Toulouse-Lautrec. Not Cézanne. You saw the film 'Moulin Rouge'? I enjoyed that because these were the scenes of my youth—Jane Avril and all the rest.

"Of course," said M. Marchal, "I'm not a dancer myself. In fact, when I was twenty, I could only do one dance."

"What's that?"

"The can-can," said M. Marchal.

M. Marchal continued thoughtfully: "I loved very much that *Belle Époque*, 1880, 1890, 1900. I sometimes find the modern epoch a little sad and dull."

He brightened. "I love great music," he said. "That is my passion. But the electric current in Vientiane has ruined my gramophone. I only hope the three trunksful of records I am sending down the Mekong to Cambodia when I make my definitive retirement will arrive safely. I have all of Wagner, Bizet's *Pearl Fishers, Carmen*—I have an adoration for *Carmen!*—Saint-Saëns, *der Rosenkavalier*—oh, that is delicious in the first scene where the old man says to the young girl, 'I am too old,' and so on, and so on."

He himself toddled rather than walked, and efforts to stop him going up the stone steps too fast were no use at all. He just sprinted ahead. Indian archaeologists had called him the Man-Goat. He literally hopped rather than climbed out of the jeep, and rode happily all the way to Phnom-Penh in it—an eight-hour trip on bumpy roads cluttered with water buffaloes, dogs, and stray Khmer sitting in the right of way. When M. Marchal came to meet you, he broke into a trot, pressed his hands together before his chest and wagged them briskly back and forth like a speeded-up Lao or Khmer salute. Once, to demonstrate the acoustics of an echoing chamber, he beat his chest like a gorilla (he would be the world's smallest and spindliest eighty-year-old gorilla).

"I still speak the Parisian argot of 1900," he said. "When I went to the Bal des Quat'z'Arts as an architecture student in 1897, the motif was Egypt, and I went just in an Egyptian bonnet and a simple robe. On purpose. Because the previous year, the theme was Gaul, and I went scrupulously dressed in rude armor, with a sword and a shield and a helmet with horns and everything. But as the evening wore on, it got hotter and hotter, and I was obliged to discard my costume." His blue eyes sparkled.

"When I first left Paris for Indochina, I was still in my twenties. When I returned in 1937, I was sixty-one. Then ten years later, at seventy-one, I came back to Angkor to restore the south gallery which had collapsed in 1946 and 1947. It took three years to rebuild it, with warriors, rhinoceroses, Hell, Paradise, garudas, and all. I've been here ever since."

M. Marchal loved pepper and fresh ginger and chocolate éclairs. He firmly refused to eat between meals, but whenever he joined me at the Grand Hôtel d'Angkor, he tucked into the *baba au rhum* and the *puits d'amour*, the *museau de boeuf* and the *cervelles vinaigrette*. "I'm used to drinking all sorts of water in all sorts of countries. When I'm in Siemreap, I always take Martini as *apéritif*. Splendid! I love all alcohols. Do you remember the vodka your friend the American anthropologist gave me in Vientiane. Excellent! But I must say, I don't like salads."

Once, apropos of nothing in particular, he turned and said, "Young man, have you ever tried opium?"

The Grand Hôtel d'Angkor offered large cool rooms with fans, and baby water beetles diving about in the glass vases filled with bougainvillaea. Outside my balcony a colony of large fruit bats clattered about in a palm tree. Lions and garudas are emblazoned on the tiles on the lobby floor. The mild and obliging Chinese airlines agent in his cubbyhole next to the desk wore a little sticker on one lens of his spectacles. And in the hotel's silver-bound guest book are the names of Sihanouk, Mountbatten, de Lattre de Tassigny, Jules Romain, Reynaud, Ely, Pineau, Prince Axel of Denmark, Hore-Belisha, Vice-President Nixon, a splendid array of Khmer, Thai and Lao princes, Malcolm MacDonald, and Miss Paris, Miss Élégance, Miss World, and Miss Riviera. Adlai Stevenson wrote, "I'll be back—I hope!" and Allen Dulles, whom we saw in the lobby looking comfortably touristic, contributed "A marvel of marvels."

Most impressed of all have been the writers. Permission was refused a group of movie makers who wanted to film a Graham Greene story at Angkor on the grounds that it would probably be full of detectives and spies and the like, inappropriate to a religious monument. Meanwhile, nobody has been able to stop the writers. Pierre Benoit's best seller of 1927, *Le Roi Lépreux,* uses Angkor as a backdrop for a faintly teasing novel of tropical passion in which the hero, Raphaël Saint-Sornin, flirts among the ruins with a royal dancer called Apsara and an American *femme fatale* called Mrs. Maxence Webb, the cousin of Admiral Jeffries who arrives in Indochina with the US battleships *Nevermore* and *Notrumps* to pay a visit to the Governor-General "which will cost several millions of dollars." Saint-Sornin is appointed Conservateur d'Angkor through influence-peddling, earning the enmity of the scholars of the École Française d'Extrême-Orient, a collection of spiteful old fuddy-duddies.

This moonshine struck me as preferable, on the whole, to André Malraux' *La Voie Royale,* published a couple of years later, which is mainly concerned with the struggles of a couple of murky men of action named Claude and Perken, sweating and swatting their way through the Indochinese jungle, bent on looting the old Khmer temples. Perken explains that "any statue at all" is worth thirty thousand francs, and a good bas-relief figure at least two hundred thousand, which comes to a good deal of money at the 1929 rate. Perken seems to be in the pay of the Thai government, but it turns out he wants to sell stolen statuary in order to buy machine guns for some tribes up across the Lao frontier where apparently he has been living as a sort of white king of the jungle. He is arming them against the conflict he feels sure is coming, though in his dark and mystical explanations of what it is all about, he says he is not sure whether the fighting will be between the colonial powers, or between them and the local people, and in what combination, or on what side his tribe will be.

Perken is present as a lost, but somehow compellingly attractive, figure. But the disturbing idea begins to emerge that for him (and the author?) violence and jungles and menacing, uncivilized types are more "real" and "true" than the humdrum everyday world. But rain forest and tribesmen are not in themselves malevolent; Malraux' jungle and its brooding, bloodthirsty villages are essentially poetical creations.

So is his Angkor and the outlying temples, here considered, surprisingly for Malraux, less as works of art than as a melodramatic stage. Archeologists and colonial civil servants are nonexistent or impossibly stuffy and obscurantist. Yet it was the French scholars and administrators, as Osbert Sitwell points out, who pushed back the border of Cambodia specifically to include Angkor and to protect it and the other temples from the Thai (and people like Perken) who were using it as a quarry.

Malraux himself, M. Marchal said one day, had come to Angkor to pick up sculpture for Parisian art dealers. He was foiled by the customs.

There is such a thing as jungle, of course, and at Ta Phrom, just to the northeast of Angkor Vat and due east of Angkor Thom, the cluster of temples and pilgrims' shelters there has been left half devoured by the vegetation to show what most of Angkor looked like when the French first arrived a century ago. The over-all impression of the stone in the forest is of gray with whitish splotches, inextricably tangled with roots and tendrils and trunks and branches, and echoing with the noise of the birds and the other animals until it seems the visitor has wandered into an aviary combined with a hot, moist glass-house in a botanical garden. It is hot and muggy, but relatively clear underfoot with the shade from the forest canopy overhead. The naga balustrades are broken, and the rectangular dark stones of the approach are buckled as though there had been an earthquake. Some of the stone is a beautiful, soft, mossy green. The roots of the banyan trees have split the great blocks of masonry, and the guidebook says ominously, "It is wise to follow the set itinerary, since some of the galleries are standing in unstable equilibrium: the necessary signs are there to warn the tourist."

Tourists come wandering into Ta Phrom from Angkor Vat, dressed for the serpentine, submarine landscape in berets, shorts, slacks, halters, movie cameras, Leicas and Rolleiflexes, and except for the hanging accessories, I am not sure that these cartoonist's costumes are not the most sensible thing to wear. The guides, when pressed, sometimes tell the visitors that one of the temples at Ta Phrom shelters a sacred cobra; this produces a delicious shudder, and cuts down the time of the tour. Most of the cobras anyone ever sees are the nagas made of stone, but there are frogs and crickets and dragonflies and small green flies and mosquitoes which can bite right through the best dimethyl-dibutylphthalate repellent.

"They don't bite me any more," said M. Marchal. "My hide has been tanned."

It was about five o'clock, and the light was fading swiftly. The great rose-chalky buttresses of the trees began to take on a theatrical, sepulchral look. A storm was blowing up in the trees high overhead where the gibbons whooped and crashed among the branches. The parakeets were raucous, and the frogs in the boggy depressions around the temples kept up an insistent *grac-grac-grac-grac-grac*. It began to thunder, and then to rain hard.

"You must realize," said M. Marchal, "that fear makes you inferior. I have adopted the Hindu philosophy: do not fear. Don't be dominated by events. Three quarters of the troubles one has are one's own fault. Even illness."

I remembered that, when teased by Lafont, he had said, "I am an Epicurean hedonist," and now he said, "I don't have religion. I take it as a philosophy. I love the philosophy of Plato and Epicurus, and also the poems of Plato. I am not a Christian. Christianity and Islam and all that is more or less recent. I mix the two greats, the Hindu and the Greek. That suffices. So far, it has served me very well.

"Buddhism is concerned with earthly life. There is nothing supernatural about it. One is reborn.

"In Hindu teaching, energy returns in different forms, a man, a turtle, a horse . . . but not as an individual.

"To me, there is no eternal life," said this man of eighty, quite cheerfully. "Nature, energy transforms itself. There is no *return* to life. We *are* a part of life. *You* are no more. You disappear completely. There are no punishments.

"In general, philosophers distinguish between matter and spirit. That is false. They are not two different things. They are different forms of the same thing.

"There is no eternity, because that presupposes a beginning. There is no beginning."

After a pause, M. Marchal said, "I am not going back to Paris. It wasn't really so good as all that. People say, 'You loved that time because you were twenty.' Perhaps that is true. I left that beautiful city to come to Indochina . . . But I shan't go back . . . My life is here now. . . ."

In a suddenly changing Laos the impact of the outside world is felt in many ways: a plane drops food to refugees in the northern mountains . . . .

supplies are parachuted to lonely outposts . . . . tribesmen wonder at marvels imported from France and Hong Kong, China, Japan and America.

*The learning of other lands
reaches the boy bonzes in the
pagodas. There are drugs
and doctors at last on the far
frontier.*

The new government surveys
the antique water buffaloes.
Tourists and taxi dancers have
come to town. . . .

and the younger generation will

come to terms with the

outside world. . . .

15 AMERICANS AND CROSSCURRENTS

BACK in Vientiane after trips to Bangkok or Saigon or Hong Kong, or even after a couple of weeks working my way through the Lao back country trying to set up CARE distributions, the capital always seemed to be sprouting change. The Lao Development Company suddenly appeared, selling Quink and Gestetner duplicating machines and Lao divinatory canes. Various rickety structures going up were said to be new hotels to rival The Bungalow, though the oldest of these efforts, belonging to a Lao friend who owned the movie house in Joy Street, had been so long in building that grass and elephant's ears and creepers were growing in the unroofed rooms which had been started first.

Always there seemed to be more American faces. And with the Americans came Thai mechanics and Chinese servants, Filipino cameramen and Japanese traders and agronomists. Every once in a while a group of promoters would turn up with plans for an international hotel for Vientiane, to be financed by American aid and staffed with talent from Hong Kong. Creating a smooth-running hotel organization with local talent obviously struck the promoters as something like trying to nail jelly to the wall.

I was against the idea on principle, but after four months of trying to find a Lao secretary-assistant, I gave in and went to Hong Kong to recruit one. I was sorry not to find a Lao. A year later the first of a bashful, newly emancipated group of Lao stenographers could be seen in odd corners of the government pecking away at their typewriters. But I was extremely lucky to find Zima Wong Wing Chow. Zima Wong was not a willowy Hong Kong secretary in a *chungsam* with a high collar and a split skirt. Rather he was a Cantonese family man about the size of a peanut, a veteran of the Burma Road where he taught mechanics, a stenographer-bookkeeper and sometime importer-exporter, who arrived in Vientiane wearing his "jungle fighting outfit," khaki clothes, a Frank Buck explorer's helmet over his ears, and knives, cups, and gear hung all over him. He had an undershot jaw and a saurian grin, and whenever he grinned he did a little sort of crouch. Sometimes he stuck his tongue out when he made a joke. He was friendly, agreeable, and obliging, and he didn't complain about sharing my room at The Bungalow, though before long he found himself better quarters. He began learning Lao and a little French on the side, and quickly brought order out of the maze of records and CARE accounts I had been struggling with. He had left his family in Hong Kong, but they would join him later.

"My wife and I have a gentlemen's agreement," said Zima. "No women."

There were relatively few Chinese in Laos—perhaps a

thousand or so members of the *Congrégation Chinoise* in the
general neighborhood of Vientiane—but you saw them everywhere, clopping along on clogs at the market, or smoking outside their small shops and restaurants which never seemed to
close. They dressed in T shirts and pajama trousers or pajama
suits. The men wore short, slightly scalped haircuts, and the
women glossy pigtails or the tight, frizzled permanent waves
America knew during the twenties. It was they and the more
numerous Vietnamese, originally brought in by the French as
middlemen, who still monopolized most of the trade. This
did not endear them, especially the Vietnamese, to their hosts,
but as usual, the Lao showed much less hostility to dominant
foreign minorities in their midst than did most of their Southeast Asian neighbors.

There were even fewer Americans in town than Vietnamese
or Chinese, but we were more conspicuous. It seemed to me,
as more and more displaced Yankees turned up, that many
of them wished devoutly that they were somewhere else. I
suppose some of them came just for the money, others because they thought it would be exciting and romantic to work
overseas, and unexpectedly found themselves at the end of
the line. The twenty-five per cent increase in pay for government service in a "hardship post" (except for career Foreign
Service officers, who are supposed to be able to take it)
seemed little enough for what they felt they had to face.
This, though, is a matter of perspective. Bangkok, which
Americans in Vientiane visited as an oasis, was also classified
as a US hardship post. I am told that after the British captured Washington during the War of 1812, the redcoats oc-
cupying the city were paid an extra sixpence a day because of
the miserably sultry climate.

With the exception of a few curious souls who set out to

learn as much about the country and its people as they could, the Americans in Vientiane were learning little French and less Lao. In the familiar dilemma of middle-class Americans (and that is most of us) overseas, they found themselves translated from the servantless city or suburb to a world overflowing with "boys" and "boyesses," most of whom were clumsy, slow, and difficult to communicate with. From a position of modest respectability, those sent overseas found themselves among a miniscule élite. It is not a specifically American dilemma. Overseas colonies of Germans, Japanese, Soviet Russians, Spaniards, American Negroes (in Liberia), Chinese, Indians, Greeks, and almost every other group one can think of back through the Romans have quickly adapted themselves to privilege if given the opportunity.

American staff people were encouraged by their chiefs to get out of town for a couple of days or so as often as possible, to avoid going stir crazy. There were usually mission chores to be done in Bangkok, Saigon, Hong Kong, or Phnom-Penh. On local leave, people could get as far afield as Manila, Tokyo, Singapore, or even Bali. But in Vientiane, unless one had some outside interests—language, ornithology, ethnology, photography, painting, history, cooking, writing memoirs, anything—life could be confining. Lao shyness only intensified Americans' withdrawal into their own circle. Listening to young, unattached, male Americans, you would think you were in the Port of Lost Men.

Not that it was really as bad as all that, though being an ignorant foreigner in a demi-Eden turning into a boom town did have its minor disadvantages. Nobody was riding herd on me in Vientiane but my own conscience. Still, there were times when the combination of CARE's eagle-eyed accounting department with its electronic machines and the charming insouciance of the Lao about getting back fifteen thousand signatures and fingerprints made me feel that my personality was in danger of splitting down the middle. The Bungalow was never exactly comfortable, and as the months grew hotter, the mothballs in my suitcases melted, and so did the batteries of candles I had stuck about the room to read and work by when the lights went out. This could be every few minutes, or for an hour or so at a time. The alleged miracle fabric of my wash-it-yourself traveling shirts was cold in winter, hot in summer, at once clammy and scratchy, and gave off sparks when being removed in the dark; in the end, I was reconverted by the *Harper's Magazine* editor, Eric Larrabee, to his own miracle fabric, cotton.

When the rains came, a rich mold flourished in my closet, and when I returned after ten days or so on the road, my cordovan shoes looked as though they were made of green suède. Swarms and legions and battalions of insects managed to get under the net, many of them no doubt still undescribed and an opportunity for an entomologist. Occasionally something went wrong with my internal machinery, but with luck whatever it was went away before anyone could find out what it was. Once after a siege of fever and chills, I was sent by the US Public Health Service doctor in town to the French military hospital; but when the lab tests failed to show signs of malaria, they all added consolingly that this wasn't conclusive, that I'd probably had a touch anyway, picked up in Indochina or Africa, and just tamped down with all the Paludrine and other antimalarial prophylactics I'd been taking faithfully over the years. Another bout, accompanied by mighty aching in the joints, sent me back to the lab, where they said that this time they thought I must have had a little dengue fever, and they couldn't find that either.

The American government missions in Vientiane were caught up in a daily struggle to fill out all the reams of paper required by Washington, and to try to find enough roofs and beds and creature comforts for the planeloads arriving to lend a hand—specialists in one field or another, or just more administrators and clerks needed to handle the growing number of administrators and clerks, under the inexorable demands of Parkinson's Law. An effort was made to drill a deep well on the grounds of the American Embassy, but all that was found was a potential salt mine. Cables led to USOM and the Embassy from a row of four large olive-drab generators in a vacant lot nearby, pounding away with a roaring, throbbing noise just like the back yard of a circus. Houses were so hard to find that the Embassy ordered aluminum cottages from Japan, and USOM wood-and-wallboard ones from Bangkok. USOM was first into the field with a compound of fourteen houses just behind the Lao Assemblée Nationale, identified on new maps as the Cité Américaine. In a nice example of Dr. Herskovits' transculturation, the Lao government was housed in pavilion-like buildings of the familiar French exposition style, while Cité Américaine were indifferent modifications of the classical bungalow, a word that means "Bengali" and a type of house on stilts that is indigenous to this part of the world. In the rainy season the Cité Américaine looks like something out of Somerset Maugham: rain cascades down the roofs and drums on the banana leaves. Ponies and cattle take shelter under the bungalows, while charcoal-gray water buffaloes attended by ubiquitous small brown boys wallow in the ephemeral lakes between the buildings, and women and little girls wade about in the water, plunging the rattan traps resembling bird cages over little fish with whiskers like catfish.

The confusions and the petty irritations—and the rewards—are much the same in Laos as in lots of other places where people are trying to pull themselves up by their own bootstraps. These are the places it has become fashionable to call "underdeveloped." Most of them are in the hot countries, and inhabited by peoples of various colors other than pinky-white. Many of the lands are naturally wealthy, but few have the means to exploit their own wealth so as to make life a little less hungry and miserable, or even to hold their own against the rising tide of population. Most of them are anxious to put Western science and technology to work, but many have misgivings at any hint of outside meddling in their own affairs. Most of these countries are ex-colonial, with all the hypersensitivity that implies, touchy vis-à-vis Occidentals, and understandably quick to sense a real or imaginary claim of privilege or an attitude of superiority.

If they are human, the sojourners must be vexed sometimes by the problems of bringing aid to far places. At home, on Capitol Hill, suspicious and vocal fellow countrymen are out with pruning shears in hand, and sometimes blood in their eye. In the field the economic missioners struggle with the red tape inherent in any government or other large organization. Also with local apathy or self-interest, lack of comprehension, and easily inflamed national sensibilities. Cut off by the language barrier, failing to understand much of the exotic, un-American culture in which they live, the visitors not surprisingly sometimes feel that their work isn't appreciated, or worse, that nobody really cares.

Some of this is a legacy from the bad old colonial days when the sahib and the memsahib sat around, taking little or no exercise, oblivious to or faintly irritated by the culture of the country, swatting insects, drinking pink gins, and developing nerves and things like "African memory." In an article on "Tropical Neurasthenia" in *Transactions of the Royal Society of Tropical Medicine and Hygiene* for 1926–27, a British physician named H. S. Stannus presented an unholy picture of the self-administered afflictions of one sort of tropical sojourner:

> exiled from home; often separated from his family, generally unable to make ends meet for some reason or other; suffering in many cases loneliness and uncongenial society; envious of others; disappointed over promotion; with ambition thwarted. Living amongst a native population causes him annoyance at every turn, because he has never troubled to understand its language and its psychology. From early morn till dewey eve he is in a state of unrest—ants at breakfast, flies at lunch, and termites for dinner, with a new species of moth every evening in his coffee. Beset all day by sodden heat, whence there is no escape, and the unceasing attentions of the voracious insect world, he is driven to bed by his lamp being extinguished by the hordes which fly at night, only to be kept awake by the reiterated cry of the brain-fever bird or the local chorus of frogs. Never at rest! Always on-guardedness.

If this is the classical bad example, and if too many of the half-million American civilians and all the others who have found themselves overseas since the end of the Second World War seem to suffer from something of the sahib mentality (this afflicts not only the Westerners but some of the Asian contingents as well), still there are encouraging signs. More and more of the Swedes and Indians and Britons and Americans one runs into in far-flung places seem to work where they do because they really want to be there, because they are alive to some of the wonder and the possibilities in the new worlds around them.

In Vientiane, where Nan MacKay and Charles Yost and Ted Tanen were among the first ashore in the American discovery of Laos, and who had some knowledge of and feeling for the new society and new limitations and opportunities, the second wave struck me as including an unfortunate preponderance of quartermasterly and clerkly souls—close relatives of Chekov's pen pushers—whose chief characteristics seemed discomfort and dismay at their new surroundings. Then, gradually, happily, there began to appear a leavening of individuals who would be a help anywhere: Perry Perregaux, who must have been a lean sixty or so, and had grandchildren to prove it, turned up as USOM agricultural adviser and an enthusiastic tennis player; his colleague Dr. William Rolston, under contract to USOM from International Voluntary Service, went into the field at Xiengkhouang with an agricultural team, and stayed there; John Standish Alden was hired fresh out of college by USOM as a village affairs man, and arrived with a knowledge of Thai, ready to shift over to Lao. Things were looking up. Hank Miller, a man of six feet six who had been the indefatigably gregarious and extremely able Voice of America chief in Hong Kong, came to Vientiane to run the US Information Service. He moved in a cloud of small Lao friends and boy bonzes, his six-year-old daughter Jenny and her Chinese chum May Ho, and their pet gibbon Dahmit. His wife Anne, a writer and a guitar player, immediately opened a bilingual school upstairs at the USIS house for the American and Chinese girls, a Lao contemporary of theirs named Ladda Sithouma, and a small Thai boy from the neighborhood.

For anyone interested, there is a fascinating lot to learn.

Laos is undoubtedly one of the most attractive, least documented lands among all the United Nations. Unlike India and England, France and Russia, China and the United States, there is not too much history to study, there are not too many books to read. There are not too many square miles to visit. It is a comfortable microcosm which one man (I am not one of them) could encompass in his time: a little world in which flow the tides of Asia and Europe and America, of faith (ideology, if you will) and technology and international experiment.

In its excellent special number "Présence du Royaume Lao," the magazine *France-Asie* in 1956 published a sixteen-page bibliography which is the most complete I have seen so far (see the drawers and stacks and shelves on any major country in the Bibliothèque Nationale, the British Museum, or the Library of Congress). With this help and with a handful of other sources—mostly just by walking around—one can begin to learn something of the character and customs and curiosities of the country. The sympathetic stranger learns to eat sticky rice, dipping into the covered rattan basket that sits before the diners, pressing a little dry but adhesive ball of the rice together, and dipping it into a clear fish sauce, stimulated with chili peppers. This, he learns, is the notorious, odoriferous, and highly nutritious *nam pa,* called *nuoc mam* in Vietnam, usually amber in color and rather like soy sauce in consistency. It is made by filtering water through ripening stacks of dried and salted fish. As with the wines of France, there are vintages and *crus* from the first, second, and third drainings, and so on. You can also eat chicken cooked in coconut milk with fennel, cinnamon, and mint; a rosy creamed Lao caviar that gets its color from stick-lac; diced raw fish marinated in lemon juice and

herbs like the Latin American *cebiche;* and a sort of Lao tar-
tar steak eaten with broth and made of beef, fish, game, or
water buffalo. To drink there is *lao,* a fire water made from
rice, or a pale, frosty-colored beer called *shoum* or *shoum-
shoum,* made from rice or corn or both and fermented in a
fat length of bamboo.

The outrageously exotic soon becomes familiar. Fish sauce
may be appreciated on both sides of the mountain spine
which runs down the Indochina peninsula, but there are more
differences than similarities on either side of this frontier
between the Indian and Chinese civilizations. Chopsticks are
used on the Chinese, but not the Indian side of the mountains.
The same sinuous mythical beasts that were dragons on the
Chinese pagodas on the Vietnamese side have here been translated into the serpents called nagas. And in Laos, as in Cambodia, sculptured nagas are as common as mice. Now an
integral part of Buddhist art and legend, the naga is a sur-
vivor of the old pre-Buddhist snake cults and animist religions, a symbol of the rainbow which unites heaven and
earth, apotheosized in the Nagaraja, the seven-headed king
of the cobras who was master of the land, and through his
daughter, the ancestor of the kings of Cambodia and Laos,
according to the common legend that runs from the south of
India up to the Indochina mountain chain. Indian, Khmer,
and Lao sculpture often shows the Buddha seated meditating
on the coils of the Nagaraja whose great hood shelters the
Enlightened One.

Lao music, a Frenchman has been quoted as saying, made
him forget "all the earth, everyone I loved, and, indeed, myself." With the loud-speakers grinding out Lao and Thai
dance music a good part of the night, and the great early
morning drums whenever there is a *boun* at the pagoda next

door (in Vientiane there is always a pagoda next door), I am inclined to agree with him. Apparently you are supposed to sleep during the day so as to be fit as a flea for the *boun*. But if you are required to do something else during the day, and the *lamvongs* won't let you sleep at night, the best thing to do is just to give up and go to the *boun*. You will be welcome.

Curious parallels used to strike me. I have always thought that Laos—with its courts of love and its bucolic-sentimental taste in popular song—must be one of the last refuges of the pastoral poetic tradition. It seems entirely probable that if the seventeenth-century British poets could have got at the Lao, they would have rechristened them all Amantha and Chloë and Amaryllis, and peopled the Lao countryside with swains and shepherdesses.

Life in Laos, "way out at the end of the West's longest and most precarious limb," as Saville R. Davis has put it in the *Christian Science Monitor*, is anything but apprehensive. A quick survey of the *bouns* would indicate, for one thing, that the kingdom must be one of the world's largest importers of colored crêpe paper and tinsel, to be made into paper chains and bright paper flowers and trees growing out of pots made of decorated beer cans, all suitable for either pagoda or secular festivities or the *boun* that is a mixture of both. And the Lao people continue to be completely, if sometimes casually, religious, with the pagoda as much a part of their daily lives as were the cathedrals of medieval Europe to the people who lived around them.

One Chinese characteristic which occurs in Laos is an enthusiastic hawking and spitting on all possible occasions; I was much relieved when a United Nations tuberculosis specialist observed that, fortunately, t.b. isn't spread by spitting in the sun—only in the shade. Something I have so far come across only among the Lao was the more engaging habit of crying in falsetto amazement: *Hooo-hooo!* and *Wheee!* and *Hooo-wheee!* I have heard fairly high ranking military men in Laos *Hoo-hoooing* and *Wheeeing* in surprise or just for the fun of it, and the effect is excellent.

As a rule, the first Lao characteristic which strikes outsiders is just plain charm. Charm is the chief national product. But the innocence that is a part of this charm can be unconsciously cruel: once I heard a great commotion and found a semicircle of smiling Lao around a tree out of which one was knocking a family of flying squirrels, for food. As they hit the ground the people beat them with sticks and whooped with glee as the animals threw themselves into ridiculous contortions and died. The squirrels might have been stuffed toys for all the connection the captors made between the beasts' feelings and their own.

Saville Davis took issue with the stereotype of the Lao as a happy child in nature, but a hopelessly indolent and inefficient fellow, and corollary conclusion that the kindest thing other people can do to the Lao is to leave them alone instead of trying to teach them skills which they can never master. He points out that chronic malnutrition is part of the answer to what looks like indolence (it was hookworm in our American South), and quotes Carter de Paul for another part of the answer: "The attitude of the Laotians is one of tranquillity and repose. Not laziness."

That there is a difference between the Lao Way of Life and that of Paris, London, or New York seems to be accepted. Under the headline ALLO, VIENTIANE, *Réalités Cambodgiennes* ran a friendly but slightly desperate two-column story complaining that the editors had hoped to fill a fair number of columns with Lao coverage and had been writing to the Lao government for a number of months asking for news and pictures, but in vain; the only material *Réalités* got was from the press officer of the Pathet Lao who regularly sent communiqués from the Communist rebel camp, in impeccable French but too long to print.

So there may be some combination of character and circumstance which makes the Lao seem charming, and a little feckless and makes-no-never-mind. But, as Davis points out with some asperity, to accept this as the basis for the conviction that the Lao are perfectly contented, though they will never be able to get anything done, and to bring in others like the Vietnamese and Chinese to do all their skilled work for them, produces little respect for the inhabitants and becomes a severely limiting factor in plans to improve their lot. He was delighted and encouraged to find gathered around Carter de Paul's dinner table compatriots who knew their jobs and liked the people in Laos with whom they worked. They told him about young Lao who were expert in the handling of milling machines and in other skills, and one of the guests commented dryly, "I have observed that the people who criticize Asians for being lazy are usually the people who sit in their chairs and expect to be waited on hand and foot."

Nothing is quite as simple as it should be, of course, and many of those who have come to appreciate the Lao still have mixed feelings about propelling them into the mechanized modern world. And though they are usually much too polite to say so, there must be days when the Lao feel some resistance, feel a little uncomfortable at being urged by foreigners to work at a faster and faster tempo. One suspects that there are times when the Lao feel they would be just as happy if the impossible were to happen, and if all these efficient strangers would go away and leave them in peace. But even if there were some imaginary, Rousseauesque way of life un-sullied by our mechanical civilization, the Lao could no longer return to it. Like many other people in odd corners of the earth these days, they have been thrown into the world to stay, like it or not.

I, for one, am extremely dubious that they would elect to go back, even if they could find a way. The independence movement in Laos may have been characteristically mod-erate, but it was a real gesture of protest against the old established order. Mr. Davis looked far enough below the surface to see that in this country with few radios and news-papers, little travel or commerce or education, still, somehow, "there are both a tangible popular opinion and informed na-tional leadership which are determined to progress." Among other things, this means schools and medicine. About half the children in the capital, reported Davis, die before they are ten years old. A USOM medical survey showed that of the ten schools in Vientiane teaching some fifty-five hundred children, half had no water supply, and half had no sanitary facilities at all, including one for twelve hundred children.

The Americans in Laos have so far been more distant than the French, but they are learning, not only about the Lao themselves but about that fascinating group of minorities who make up a majority in the kingdom. Individual Ameri-cans are in Laos for different reasons, but I think it's fair to say that, except for a handful of missionaries and scholars and artists and a few others, most Americans and other foreigners —agronomists and all—are ultimately in Laos for political reasons. Members of the American government missions have been racing against time to try to create in Laos a nation strong enough to resist the attractions and pressures across the Communist frontiers to the north. Since the Vietminh invasions of Laos and the Geneva truce, there has been fear in Washington that if Laos were to fall to the Communists, then Thailand, Burma, Cambodia, and Malaya would all go toppling after it.

Whatever the future of Laos, whether it remains in the French Union or not, it surely will do its best to run its own affairs.

Chinese aid for Laos, perhaps followed by other Communist and neutralist aid *à la Cambodge*, seems to be in the cards.

"Laos is a small country," said Prince Souvanna Phouma during his trip to Peking in the summer of 1956, "but it is aware of the duties deriving from its geographical position, and it would not do anything that could be regarded as a threat by its neighbors." The accord then signed by Souvanna Phouma and Chou En-lai called for (1) Lao neutrality, avoidance of military alliances "as long as its security is not menaced," and a ban of foreign military bases on its territory, other than provided for in the Geneva Agreement; (2) support of this policy by the People's Republic of China; (3) observance by both countries of the Indian-Chinese five principles of peaceful co-existence, and the promotion of friendly relations between the local authorities on both sides of the Lao-Chinese frontier; and (4) development of Lao-Chinese economic and cultural relations.

There has been no sudden burgeoning of trade between China and Laos since the accord was signed, nor a rush of Lao and Chinese dancers, painters, and scholars back and forth, nor much of anything except the collection of Shanghai

Commercial Press reprints in the Vientiane museum. But with the outbreak of fraternity, the possibility of an additional source of foreign aid, and the Pathet Lao working toward integration with the Royal Government and a place within it, with the Lao leaders' awareness of the awesome six hundred million across their northern frontier, there will be new sources of strength for the cause of Communism in the Land of the Million Elephants. Through the years of ambush and sniping and skirmish when the Pathet Lao refused to let go of the two northern provinces, the sorely tried Royal Government, who couldn't get so much as a postman into the area, gently referred to the rebels as "the Lao who were not at the side of the Royal Lao forces during the hostilities." When the almost interminable political minuet of discussions between the Royal Government and the Pathet Lao were finally to cease, and the Pathet Lao were to give up their army and their provinces for the respectability of a legal political party, the Neo Lao Haksat, and two portfolios in the Cabinet, they emerged with the Ministries of Religion & Fine Arts and of Economic Planning, Reconstruction & Urbanization, the latter including American aid and reserved for Prince Souphannouvong, Souvanna Phouma's smoothly handsome half brother who is the old Pathet irreconcilable with strong friends in Peking and Hanoi. The smiling Prince Souphannouvong announced to the United Press that he would follow a policy of co-operation with the United States, since Laos needed aid "not for several years, but for several decades."

Looking back later, and from a little distance, I imagine that the strength of the Communist-oriented Neo Lao Haksat, especially in rural areas, in the supplementary parliamentary elections which were finally held must have been a shock to

American and some other foreign observers in Laos, who had anticipated a more conservative countryside. The respected *Hindu* of Madras welcomed progress toward integration as showing that "given sufficient goodwill and patience, settlements between Communist and non-Communist groups can be achieved." The London *Economist* now called Laos a "show-case for co-existence," and expected that the Lao experiment of working with the Communists would be studied closely in places like Burma and Malaya. The Delhi critical weekly *Thought* was not so sanguine, and feared that "the Communist Prince Souphannouvong now occupies a place of far greater strategic import than he did as leader of the straggling Pathet Lao forces. . . ."

But this was all still in the future the year I lived in Laos. Like the blue-brown islands and the headlands of the South China Coast, covered with mist, dense sometimes, drifting, dissipating for a moment, and revealing before closing in again the top of a hill or mountain, a bit of a bay, a ghostly sail, the future of Laos seemed obscure, parts of it hidden, parts vaguely suggested. No matter what may happen, I expect that it will be a good many years before the metamorphosis of Lan Xan is complete.

Few Lao whom I met were so inconsiderate of others' feelings that they objected if they were not in agreement with something which seemed important to the guest, the foreigner. There was one notable exception: a senior Lao army officer in the north of the country who expressed himself pretty freely about things which we both tacitly assumed were important to all of us. No doubt he aired some of his own crochets, but I had the feeling that he spoke for a number of basically friendly but unheard-from people in the kingdom who were dissenters on some score, who had qualifications or modifications or improvements to offer.

"Aid should be used to the last ounce," he said, "but you should give aid for the brain, too."

He had a stubbly, thin mustache, a flat face, and hair parted in the middle, which gave him a rather old-fashioned look. He was wearing a white singlet with white shorts and white tennis shoes. His short, thick eyebrows bounded up and down as he talked.

"When *you* come to Vientiane, you worry first about the plumbing and your quarters. You seclude yourselves. You yearn for Paris or London or Rome. You are only here for a year or so. And this place is full of mosquitoes and smells and night soil, and the food is so expensive and so uninteresting.

"But on the other side, for *them*, it is the work of a lifetime, a matter of life and death. They work all day, every day, and this is how they win.

"We think those with power must have the best of everything. When the French visited a village, they got the best girls, the best pigs, the best chickens, the best of everything. When a Vietnamese agent reaches a village, he doesn't take the most beautiful girls or the chickens or the pigs. He stays outside the village, and helps work in the fields and harvest the rice.

"On one side, you have four thousand years of feudalism, and on the other, people all over the country have been excited and tempted to leave their brothers and their fathers and their families, and join the Pathet Lao.

"When you dump a lot of money in at the top, then it turns to poison. It can be used against you, like the American weapons you gave the police in south Thailand to combat the Communist guerillas from Malaya. They were sold to the Communist guerillas. If you give arms and ammunition to an army without a cause to fight for, in the end they will turn on you like the Chinese. We must, we must give them food for their brains, give them something to believe in."

16 TROUBLE

In Southeast Asia, in Laos, in Vientiane, and in The Bungalow, things seemed to be going from bad to worse. After nearly a year we had done so little when there was so much to do. Here I was, still struggling with planes that were requisitioned, pirogues that didn't arrive, roads that didn't exist, with pettifogging public officials. There were endless daily stratagems designed to try to get a room and office space outside The Bungalow, or just to try to get my laundry back. Each day I seemed to be less aware of the beauty of the world around me and the great graciousness of the people among whom I lived. Suddenly I became more and more concerned with all the miserable, niggling little things that went wrong. More and more I felt like a man trying to run under water.

For one thing, I didn't feel at all well. I lay down one night after supper, watching the great three-bladed fan slowly revolving overhead, and gloomily considered Max Finger's dictum: "There are only two kinds of Americans in Laos— those who have amoebic dysentry, and those who don't know it." The smell of drains drifted over the cracked ochre wood-work of my room, and the holes in the outside door were stuffed with plugs of paper and cotton. In the daytime, when I opened the wardrobe door, a great cloud of mosquitoes boiled out of their dark refuge. Fungicides and other unguents melted into thin liquids in their pots, and the battery of can-dles on the bronze drum drooped limply in the heat.

I thought gloomily of the Pathet Lao in the north, then still protesting their patriotism and loyalty to a united Laos, sending down delegations for endless palavers with the Royal Government, talking and talking and talking as did the Com-munist negotiators at Panmunjom, eating the miserable ban-quets downstairs in The Bungalow's dining room, toasting peace and unity, and then going back to Phongsaly and Sam-neua which they continued to rule by force of arms, in defiance of the government. Behind them were the Vietminh of Hanoi and Peking's Communist government commanding 630 mil-lion industrious, highly intelligent people. No doubt if Peking and Moscow decided it were in the general interest of the in-ternational Communist movement, the Pathet Lao would be sacrificed as was the German Communist party in the thirties, there would be no more outside support for them, and we would have integration of the two lost Lao provinces the day after tomorrow. At the moment, this seemed a fairly slender hope to cherish.

The Chinese colony in Laos was fairly small, but no one was very much surprised to learn that someone had introduced Chinese Communist textbooks in their schools. As opposed to this, the American emergency refugee relief program, which was supposed to admit four thousand Chinese over three years from Southeast Asia (out of a world refugee quota of 113,000 refugees), turned up in Laos in the person of a US civil servant who spent an afternoon considering the problem, did not let the American Embassy know in advance of his visit, came to see me because someone had given him my name, and was only with great difficulty persuaded to talk to a representative of the Overseas Chinese community in Vientiane. As a result of things like this there were no refugee visas at all for the three Indochinese states, Thailand, Burma, Indonesia, and the Philippines where live several millions of Chinese, while a thousand visas, or twenty-five per cent of the quota, were given to Japanese, who apparently had been suddenly metamorphosed into "refugees" because they were needed by fruit growers in California. This didn't seem to be much of a counterattraction to the Communist love-and-friendship campaign.

Among my fellow countrymen in Laos, few of the economic missioners whom I'd lately met seemed enthusiastic about their jobs, or had much faith in the future of what they were doing. I found this depressing. Most of the fifty-odd million dollars a year of United States aid went to the Lao Army, but of the ten to thirteen millions spent annually on economic development, the eight millions being spent over a two-year period by France, and the nearly four millions' worth of equipment to come from the Colombo Plan, there wasn't much visible yet except a few French teachers in the *lycées*, and an American road that didn't get too far out of town. The swarms of middle and lower echelon Americans involved in economic aid seemed enmeshed in the endless housekeeping, personnel, and supply problems of their own missions—as were we all to a degree—but the fight for quarters, the difficulties in getting

furniture and food and other supplies flown in, the infinity of
the reports demanded by Washington, all seemed to take up
so much time and strength that there appeared to be little
time left in which to get on with the job. Some of the economic
missioners whom I met were so preoccupied by the little world
in which they lived that at times I doubted they were really
in Laos.

All this was not the end of the world, but I suddenly found
myself becoming more and more discouraged. To cheer up
I went to a small party given by a couple of embassy secretaries, the endlessly ebullient Elaine Hefferman and Carol
Moran, and there tried to drink a scotch and soda, but it tasted
unaccountably bitter, and I could only get through half of it.
Some of us went on to the Circle Privé de Vientiane where a
number of young French *colons* and Lao friends were revolving in a *lamvong* in a room darkened except for a few red
lights. We moved on to a couple of the Vientiane honky-tonks
which had mushroomed with the easy money flowing in with
foreign aid. In one there was a good Vietnamese band with a
clean trumpet, playing "Babalu," the old Afro-Cuban classic,
and too many people on a small dance floor—rather like New
York, except that outside was the Mekong, and shining in the
moonlight, the great Buddha in the ruins of Phya Vat. In another hall-like shack there was a French musette band with
jazzbo lumberjack shirts, playing *paso dobles* and "Quizas,
Quizas, Quizas," Saigon taxi girls with cribs out back, a few
more young Frenchmen who looked like beachcombers,
deeply sunburned, with rolled-up sleeves, and scraggly blond
mustaches and duck-tail haircuts. There were occasional
fights. I sat with my friends, under the ghastly glare of a pressure lamp, trying to get down a few salted peanuts (57 cents

for a few in a tiny saucer) without much success. As a cure for
melancholia, Vientiane night life was not working.

The next day I felt terrible. Friends at USIS asked me to
pilot an American lady lecturer around the town, and I had to
lean on the wheel of the jeep for a couple of minutes in a fit of
gagging before we got under way. She looked at me curiously,
but was kind about it. That afternoon at the dispensary behind
the American Embassy, I was told I'd probably been taking
the wrong kind of antimalarial prophylactic, one which sometimes induces nausea. But I continued to feel feverish, more
and more nauseated and gloomier and gloomier, and finally
took to my stained mosquito net in the shambles of The Bungalow, asking Zima to try to find a doctor.

The American missions' doctor came that evening, took a
few samples of me, looked at my eyeballs, and promised to
return the next day with the results of the lab tests at the
French military hospital. When he returned, he told me gently
that I had come down with a severe case of infectious hepatitis, and went off to ask for permission to get me evacuated to
Bangkok in the military attaché's plane, which was leaving
for Bangkok before any commercial flight. This was a round
for him, for he had long objected to my eating Lao food
upcountry. I later gathered from Wells Klein that the doctor
was seconded by a chorus of "I told you so's" after I was carried out of Vientiane. The doctor had recommended that
when traveling in the provinces, I should live on US Army
K-rations. I was happy that there were no K-rations available.
And more than one of my friends had been poisoned on the
beefsteak in the capitol's most elegant restaurant. Also, the
doctor was the second of two American government physicians
who had to be removed, more or less by force, from Laos,

suffering from congenital, multiple allergic reactions to their surroundings. But that's another story. Now, the doctor was kinder than he ever had been, and I was grateful that he was there and knew what to do with me.

Bumping out to the airport the next morning in the jeep with Zima, with the knowledge I might not be coming back for some time, if ever, my nose tickled, and as when I was leaving New York to come to Laos, I suddenly saw everything in stereopticon perspective: the early morning mists and the water buffaloes along the road, the workmen on the tiled roof of a pagoda where the lights and paper streamers and dancing platform were being made ready for one of the first *bouns* of the new season, the stocky little Lao paratroopers in their berets at the airport, off for a jump somewhere in this still unsettled country. The pilot helped me climb into the small plane, we were off, and I wasn't to come back for a long time.

17 THE BANGKOK NURSING HOME AND THE WORLD

THE next five weeks I spent tranquilly, flat on my back in the Bangkok Nursing Home on Convent Road. The sky was clear now in early autumn at the end of the rainy season, and in the gardens leading away from the terrace outside my room the sun was gentle on the flowering trees: waxy white and pink frangipani, hibiscus, gardenia and jacaranda, and flame-of-the-forest like a burst of Chinese firecrackers. After dark, the white trumpets of the moonflowers opened on the moonflower tree just opposite my room.

Mynahs like clerical dignitaries stalked about the lawn, and sometimes there was a flash of metallic blue-green that looked like a kingfisher but was called a jay. I was visited by squadrons of cherry-colored dragonflies.

I seemed to be lying in bed in a country house, late on a sunny Sunday morning. The world of Bangkok and Southeast Asia was far away: the shimmering spires of the Temple of the Dawn and the launch-loads of tourists nosing their way through the floating market, the lines of seated Buddhas shining dull gold in the dim pagodas; and further off, the Pathet Lao in their northern mountains, and the plastic bombs in Saigon.

Once the first few hospital days were over and I began to look a little less yellow around the eyeball and was no longer being fed glucose through a vein in my arm, things began to look better.

Acute depression is a common enough symptom of hepatitis, and it was a relief to discover that the mists of melancholia which had been gathering over me until I was weary of everything and everybody in the country, including myself, were a reflection neither of my mind nor heart, but of my liver.

The little Thai and Chinese nurses were merry and efficient. There was Miss Sri and Miss Pranom, and Miss Duangthippe. Miss Surat, who was cheerful and solid, customarily came bustling in with the threat: "You be good or I cut off your head!" It was she who stuck her head in the door one day when I was still saffron, and hissed confidentially, "You want to see a tapeworm?" I tried to say "No," but it didn't do any good. The tapeworm was very long and thin and in its white enameled basin, even yellower than I was, which Miss Surat seemed to feel should cheer me up.

There was a competent staff including a British matron and two British nurses, a Danish doctor, Thai doctors, and an American Air Force doctor attached to the local embassy who had seen so many cases of infectious hepatitis, amoebic hepatitis, and homologous hepatitis that he considered himself a patron saint of the affliction. All of these people assured me that, in spite of a severe infection, I had an excellent chance of recovery. They said that there were relatively few fatalities.

Unless, of course, there were complications. When I asked about the USIS officer from Saigon who had recently succumbed, I was told that there must have been complications. Then a Bangkok government dredging official turned up in the next room, also suffering from hepatitis, and early one morning he died, gasping terribly. Everyone agreed that there had been complications, but I felt chastened and disinclined to count on anything.

In the hospital all the outside world, frivolous or serious, seemed real enough but a little distant. It was as though I were floating slowly over Southeast Asia in a balloon. Altogether, it was a reflective sort of time, a good time and place to try to think about what had happened during the past year, to take stock and try to work out what I and all of us as foreigners thought we were doing so far away from home, what seemed to make sense and what didn't.

The air around my hospital bed and above the flowering trees seemed full of questions, more questions than answers:

Do people really care, are they really grateful when other people try to help them? And does it really matter a hoot whether they are grateful or not? This one wasn't too hard. It seems to me that if people—without prodding—do feel thankful, well then, so much the better, for it is warm and encouraging. But if we as a people want to try to help some of the other people in this world (Motivated perhaps by a bewildering mixture of sympathy, enlightened self-interest, humanitarianism, missionary impulses, desire to share, wanting to do something useful, and just plain politics), then it seems silly to feel hurt if people don't fall on their knees and sob with gratitude. Often they are annoyed. They don't like to be preached at, and they step on their benefactors' toes. It may be a little hard on the benefactors sometimes, but in the end, just the fact that there is need and distress and a chance, a very small chance, to do something about it, ought to be reason enough.

Gratitude and appreciation are like happiness: they cannot be purchased and they cannot be pursued directly. It not only is rude to demand thanks while trying to help someone, as some of our legislators seem to expect, it just doesn't work. It is like the insistent "Do you love me? Do you love me? Do you love me? Tell me that you love me" that drives out love. The feeling of warmth and gratitude comes by itself, unbidden, from the most touching and unlikely places and at the most unexpected times. But you can't chase it.

More to the point than demanding pledges of affection is the selection of people to go overseas who will get along there. To send overseas a man who has scant respect for the people and the place where he is going, who is unwilling to learn something of his new surroundings and who frets that everything isn't the same as it is at home in Grand Rapids, Michigan (that is fair—I was born there), is almost worse than not sending anyone at all. There are now about two million Americans overseas, of whom a half million are civilians. We have always been blessed with some really outstanding representatives—Benjamin Franklin was one of the best. And certainly among the Americans overseas are some outstandingly able people, far more it seems to me than when I began to travel, at the end of the Second World War. Then one of our veteran ambassadors assured me earnestly that, while there might be a few cranks and soreheads, almost everybody in the world loved and trusted the United States. I wish this were true, but it just isn't always so, and it wasn't especially so at the ambassador's own post.

Now there is a whole new race—Americans overseas—coming into being. *Life* devoted a special double number in the winter of 1958 to this new breed, and for the first time the international edition ran more pages of copy than its domestic parent.

Sometimes I think of the new species as the seersucker men, but beyond the Brooks cord suits, the correct short haircuts, the finned monster cars, and the commissaries with all the comforts of home from hominy grits to good bourbon, there are increasing numbers of people who are both sympathetic and intelligent and willing to learn something of the world around them. Unfortunately there still are too many whose horizons are sharply limited by bugs and natives, who's got what housing, and their rascally servants (they never had any before, and now it's the biggest thing in their lives). A two-year tour becomes twenty-four months of complaint.

I think that the best hope for American efforts overseas lies in far more careful selection of the people who are shipped out, both the government people and the private people, and at least minimum preparation for the new worlds in which they will live: In India the American Embassy's indoctrination course in the Indian way of life, arts, history, politics, and general background, begun under Ambassador Bowles and continued since then, has been a marked success. By contrast, there is no such opportunity to learn in many posts, or while training in the United States. In Cambodia, where there is no such course, an experienced American information officer whom we met there reported that she had been given a couple of weeks' preparatory training in Washington, of which all but a day or so were devoted to the recognition of Communism. Cambodian background she was supposed to "pick up on the spot." It may be that an experienced observer with an inquiring mind would do just that, but it's a good deal to ask of the average transplanted technical man or suburban housewife, both of whom are members of the American community, and with a fair amount of influence, good or bad.

It was noticeable that most of the Americans I ran into in Indochina spoke neither Lao, Cambodian, Vietnamese, or even French, nor were they attempting to learn. Nor were they being asked to do so. I am embarrassed to say that I learned very little Lao, and it is not difficult. We can do better than that. Mr. Bowles has suggested that technicians and others to be sent overseas be trained in the language, history, economy, social structure and government of the areas where they will work, as well as in their own specialities. If good small general and reference libraries were maintained in each country by the embassies and economic missions, it would help a lot. A book or so of required reading might not be a bad idea. In his *Ambassador's Report,* Bowles noted that Russian technicians at a Chinese airfield were reported by Indian visitors to live in the same quarters and to eat the same food as the Chinese, to speak Chinese, and to clean their own latrines. This is not always true of Russian technicians, who can be as aloof as anybody, but in this case they seem to have convinced the visitors that they were dedicated spirits.

Americans have no monopoly on xenophobia and provincialism. When Communist China began to lecture itself on "Great Nation Chauvinism," which is just another name for the classical conviction that all non-Chinese are foreign devils, it was opening up a rich field for improvement.

Some observant and disrespectful person one day is going to be able to point to a number of superficial similarities between the Yanks and the Soviets overseas. Or for that matter, similarities with Indian, Japanese, UN personnel and all overseas contingents, who by their very nature become a sort of élite. I have sometimes been reminded of the similarities of the old-fashioned colonial mentality I used to keep running into in parts of Africa and around the Caribbean—the sort of person who keeps assuring you that "natives" are "just down out of the trees"—they could be Dutch or British, French or American, but they all believed in large pools of poorly paid labor, living at a subsistence level, with little education and less politics. Soviet attitudes toward their own underdeveloped areas are reminiscent of these old colonials at several points. Yet at an international exposition in Delhi, where the Americans worked through interpreters, the Russians showed up in force speaking several Indian languages.

This is not to say that just because the Soviet missionaries turn up speaking fluent Swahili or Mandarin, their own background will not be the essentially narrow one provided by their technical schools. But the importance of learning languages is hard to overestimate.

I was lying there in the hospital thinking about some of these things, watching the Siamese birds and the flowering trees and thinking I really ought to get some work done, when Wells Klein came zooming in from Saigon. Paul Gordon, our regional chief, a big, tough but gentle man who had once directed agriculture in Iran, had brought reindeer to Alaska, and who had helped colonize Canton and Enderbury Islands in the course of a long and distinguished career overseas, had now fallen downstairs with a chest of drawers on top of him, and was in the hospital for major repairs. This left Wells trying to run an efficient distribution in the midst of a small civil war in Vietnam, while commuting to Hong Kong to talk to Paul Gordon in the hospital and work with the CARE refugee program there, to Bangkok to untangle incoming shipments to help me try to run Laos by remote control, then to Vientiane to hold the fort with Zima Wong Wing Chow. He did a remarkable job.

After Wells and I had had a chance to sort things out a bit, Pamela Tadman, who was one of the two British nurses in the place, turned up off duty at three o'clock, and promptly abducted Wells to take her to a rugby game. After they had gone, I began to think of the really good and useful and cheerful people I had met working outside their own countries—more and more of them. In the case of Pamela, a browned and bouncy girl who was one of the more decorative features of the pool at the Royal Bangkok Sports Club—she had been brought up in the rectory of an English village where the house had always been full of Thai students. She was so taken by their stories that she came out to Thailand as a nurse, and a year after her arrival, imported a neighbor named Patricia Mackay, equally jolly and equally curious to see other people in other parts of the world. Pat industriously learned the names of the trees and flowers and birds in town, and I managed to learn some of them from her. The two girls between them seemed to be on good terms with half of Bangkok, Thai and international. Wells Klein, on the other hand, was headed back to school. He planned to work for his doctorate in anthropology at Cornell, then head out again. He would be remarkably well qualified, a Ph.D. at thirty-three who had already had five years of hard experience in the field behind him, in charge of the feeding of 2½ million Yugoslavs during a period of famine, and working with the refugees during the great exodus from North to South Vietnam.

I remembered an attractive young couple called Pete and Pet Pettingill who had helped teach Ethiopians how to publish their own schoolbooks, and who had done such a good job for USIS in Monrovia that the Liberians were distinctly annoyed when Washington insisted on bringing them home over local protests. Then there was the Maryknoll father whom I met near Lake Titicaca where he had been tough-minded enough to remove all the statues of the saints from his small church until his Andean Indian parishioners could be brought to understand the symbolism, and accept the disappointing fact that there was no magic in the plaster; he also ran a dispensary and a school and learned the language, as any good missionary should—medical, religious, or socio-economic. I later came to know a co-religionist of his in Calcutta, a Mother Teresa who many years ago had come from Albania but now was Indian, who ran dispensaries and schools for the poorest of the poor, and in the crawling slums of Kalighat in back of the Temple of Kali, the goddess of destruction, had founded a Home for the Destitute Dying, where people were carried in off the streets so that at least they might leave this world with some dignity, in a relatively clean place with fewer flies, a little plain food, and someone there who cared for them.

All of those people whom I had admired (and beside whom I usually felt slightly useless) came crowding back. From my own country there were the heartening number of people from the South, and the Deep South at that, who with no trace of condescension were happy living and working with the people of Haiti, Ethiopia, and Liberia.

I believe we could cast a much wider net. America, for one, is full of young people, and numbers of older ones, who have the qualifications of intelligence, enthusiasm, interest in other peoples and other ways and a desire to get to know them better, and who would give their eyeteeth for a chance to work overseas—this at the same time that government and private groups seem to have great difficulty in finding hardy souls to send abroad, and when it is felt that they must be offered premiums and perquisites to live in a "hardship post" like Bangkok. The late Karl Patterson Schmidt, an old friend who was Curator of Zoölogy at the Chicago Natural History Museum, suggested in *Harper's Magazine* a few years ago that consulates in green hells and desert outposts be manned by naturalists and anthropologists and others who find such places congenial. Many variations on this theme are possible, and I am convinced one could find appropriate talent in the most unexpected places. I am also convinced that a dash of unorthodoxy—just a dash—would do our conformist services no harm.

I dreamed of some of the happy mavericks who had crossed my path: Yale Richmond and Doc Slusser beating their ways through the Laotian hinterland, and learning more about that deceptively easy country than all the earnest, intelligent, and desk-bound analysts at the center would ever know. Yale observed: "You should point out that we are working in these countries to further American foreign policy, and an anthropologist, or other student of an area, will not help American foreign policy unless he has what I call political savvy. What we need is a combination of the two types. Someone who is interested in the area, who is sensitive to the people there, who can help them, but who is also cognizant of the issues as they relate to American foreign policy. This rare bird is hard to find."

Page, who later covered the same country on a bicycle, with a broken foot, and covered it well, photographed the Lao and the Africans with the same affection and respect with which he had photographed the bums of Third Avenue and the American white-collar worker.

None of these people fitted into neat little boxes; all of them shared something of the quality which made someone refer to another photographer, Robert Capa, as "the man who invented himself."

Especially Dr. Dooley. Or perhaps he is beyond classification. He may have left some of the American colony in Vientiane in a state of shock compounded of indignation, amazement, dismay, awe, and envy. But there is no indication the Lao ever felt any of this, and the important point is that he did run a small hospital for a year in a part of northern Laos that desperately needed one. He had written a book called *Deliver Us from Evil,* about the evacuation from Haiphong in North Vietnam, where he had been a young US Navy doctor. Some of the Americans now in Laos who had also been through the evacuation objected that Dr. Dooley left the impression he had been up there stemming the Red tide single-handed. As he moved from the United States to Laos, he paused for frequent press conferences where he announced that he would push on to parts where no white man had ever trod before. Actually I met Dooley for the first time somewhat later, in Hong Kong, while he was on his way to these wonderful places, and we had a good lunch while he outlined his plans. With a considerable sum of money he had made in royalties from his Haiphong book, he was taking three of his old medical corpsmen to Laos. They would jeep into a primitive village in the late afternoon; then, in the dusk, he and his corpsmen would toss a baseball around, limbering up. Gradually the villagers would edge forward and become interested; soon they would all be tossing a ball around; he would show them Technicolor cartoons specially supplied to Dr. Dooley by Walt Disney, and the first thing you knew, the Lao would be learning about the American way of life, the medical team would be stamping out yaws and malaria, and training midwives.

Dr. Tom Dooley is driving, exuberant, and he looks like a clean-cut, all-American boy. His dress is sharp Ivy League. At lunch he said, "Did I ever tell you how the Communists pushed my mother downstairs in Scranton, Pa.?"

"Yes, you did, Tom. About ten minutes ago."

"Well, it was like this. I was speaking in Scranton and my mother was there, and a man disguised in priest's clothes jostled my mother at the top of some stairs . . . " He described how his mother had been injured falling downstairs.

In a moment he asked, "Did I tell you about the cable Dr. Schweitzer sent me?"

"Yes, Tom. Three times."

"Well, Dr. Schweitzer cabled me and said, DOCTOR TOM YOU WILL ALWAYS BE HAPPY BECAUSE . . ."

This sort of thing had the members of the Hong Kong Foreign Correspondents Club climbing straight up the walls. But I noticed that they gave Dooley plenty of space in their dispatches. He always said something quotable.

The last time I saw him, Tom Dooley was still talking about "jungles," "natives," and "witch doctors" and other relics of the nineteenth century and the Sunday supplements. But he had done what few foreigners in Vientiane believed he would do: keep his small hospital in a remote Lao village going for a year. Some people complained that his corpsmen, who had little more than extensive first-aid training, were attempting difficult operations. But I have been in too many places where anybody arriving with a bottle of merthiolate and a few gauze bandages was a medical miracle not to feel that this was an improvement.

Dr. Dooley was all spruced up and on his way back to the

United States and the women's club lecture circuit where he would try to raise enough money to return to Laos and open another hospital in another village. On his way back, he said, he planned to dedicate his life for six weeks to helping Dr. Schweitzer at Lambaréné in French Equatorial Africa, and while there would write a book about his adventures in Laos which he would sell to the *Reader's Digest*. He has done it by this time, too. He finished it before I got to the end of this chapter. Never mind. In spite of the drum beating and all this business about the great white healer, I like Dr. Dooley, and I am glad he chose Laos.

Zima Wong commuted between The Bungalow in Vientiane and the Bangkok Nursing Home lugging a file almost as big as himself, sprouting Consolidated Inventory Reports, letters to donors, Disbursement Report Memos, Vessel Outturn Reports, Discursive Reports, and cables. He bent earnestly over his stenographer's Eye-Ease Spiral Notebook, taking the seventeenth memorandum for an agricultural officer asking where were the specifications, or even snapshots, of the hand tools his ministry four months ago said it needed urgently. Zima grinned like a gavial, reported that standards at The Bungalow were slipping, and brought news of people with whom we worked in Laos.

Because the doughty DC-3 on charter from CAT to the local American embassies and economic missions was still making the twice-weekly milk run, Saigon-Phnom Penh-Bangkok-Vientiane and return, I saw a fair number of diplomats, anthropologists, newspapermen, and others who were permitted to hitch a ride on the plane, cargo permitting, and who often dropped in to see if I were still surviving as they came in from the backwoods to make the rounds of Bangkok and take back a few supplies. (No Lao ever came to see me;

perhaps some started out, but they didn't make it.) My visitors and I talked about American aid or other people's aid, what seemed to be the right approach and what the wrong one, what the rôle of the individual might be in all this. I may say that we were very free with our opinions, from the security of our position of not having to make many of the decisions.

We talked about the few small successes and the many frustrating failures encountered by any individual setting out to do a job in a far corner of the world. We speculated on the adventureousness or humanitarianism or political pressures or need for a good steady job, which led to so many citizens' laboring so mightily with such miniscule effect in some forgotten land back of the beyond which few of them had ever heard of before. We were not trying to minimize the really excellent work of many thousands of Americans and others overseas—particularly some of the professional Foreign Service officers and the information people. Not all expatriates are indifferent to their surroundings—particularly when they are encouraged not to be so. Mary Slusser wrote later from Belgrade that roughly half the Americans there were learning Serbo-Croatian. Rather we were concerned with the places and people and things which could stand a little improvement.

Some of us were concerned over what seemed to be the short-range philosophy of American aid, with its evangelistic overtones, the heavy imbalance of military over economic programs, its instinctive alliance with economic and political orthodoxy even when this meant shoring up corrupt, authoritarian local leaders at the risk of having American aid tarred with the same brush. Chester Bowles has tartly characterized the philosophy of the frightened with, "How silly we must seem reducing every question to the Communist equation.

Some of the questions are bigger than Communism. . . .
Point Four . . . is potentially far bigger than Communism.
If all the Communists on earth disappeared overnight, the
need for foreign aid to assist new struggling peoples to achieve
stable democratic societies would still be there." In his report on his mission to India, I think Mr. Bowles put his finger
on most of the basic points when he wrote:

"It is essential that we ask ourselves some blunt questions
about our real objective in extending Point Four aid in Asia
and Africa.

"Is it to make America popular?
Is it to buy the people's gratitude?
Is it to win allies in the Cold War?
Is it to increase the acceptance of capitalism abroad?

"Most of these objectives, like stopping Communism, are
desirable in themselves, but if we make them the direct
essential goals of our foreign aid I am confident that we will
achieve none of them.

"As I see it our primary objective is to strengthen democracy
in the new free nations of Asia for its own sake, without
regard to occasional disagreements with them which are
certain to rise.

Democracy presupposes disagreements, and it is democracy to which we as a nation are above all committed."

To this objective of strengthening democracy, I would
add another that seems to me to be just as important—at least
for the private organizations whose people-to-people aid programs Mr. Bowles approves: aid just because aid is needed.
Russian and other Communist-bloc aid programs now shift-
ing into high gear seem to me to suffer from the same re-

strictive, short-range sort of thinking as our own, except more so. "No strings!"—they do protest too much. The Communists have every appearance of expecting a quick politico-economic return on their investments. United Nations technical assistance and the multi-national Colombo Plan, though both considerably smaller than the big national efforts, seem to escape the restrictive hand of self-interest, as do the extremely useful private programs of the Rockefeller and Ford Foundations. There are some indications that the rôle of the private and especially the international organizations will grow, and that the United States and other great powers who have so far shied away from the idea may find it more practical to channel increasing amounts of their assistance through the UN in order to avoid the mistrust and resistance to co-operation that is the legacy of colonialism in any of the newly independent, but in some ways still dependent, countries.

The fact that these touchy points are being discussed at home and in the field, the increasing acceptance of the fact that ideas as well as armies are a force to be reckoned with, the concern with the very different attitudes and emotions of other peoples, an increasing awareness in the West that gadgets are not an end in themselves but tools in a life whose course and purpose are the main concern of man, all these have put a slight dent in the old simplification that the East is "spiritual" and the West is "materialist." A growing number of people are aware that Gandhi in South Africa, perfecting the campaign of passive resistance that was to win independence for India, was deeply influenced by Thoreau's essay "On the Duty of Civil Disobedience" and by his correspondence with Tolstoi. And—wheels within wheels—Thoreau himself had earlier been influenced by classical Indian philosophy. Also, a few people at least have become aware of the ironical fact that in a year and a half in Indo-china the United States spent more money in support of the French forces there than she had for the whole of France under the successful Marshall Plan, and still the French lost against the Vietnamese who had been fired with the idea of independence.

Reading the Bangkok papers every day and listening to visitors' gaudy tales—mostly true—of plunder in the local government, brought one face to face with the problem of how to administer a foreign aid program in an imperfect world with a fair number of black sheep governments among the family of nations. Some foreigners in Bangkok, remembering the same politicos' enthusiastic membership in the Axis, had reservations about the then government's protestations of military and moral solidarity with the free world. It was obvious that a good deal of foreign aid money being pumped in at the top simply wasn't trickling down. But the head of the government before that one, General Pridi Banomyond, who, like Ho Chi Minh in Indochina, was supported by the US in the war against Japan, is now up in Communist China's "Free Thai Autonomous Republic" where he claims an army of thirty thousand, presumably ready to "liberate" their oppressed cousins to the south whenever politically expedient. Where to turn? Both Thai governments have since been toppled by *coups d'état,* and we shall see what happens to the next ones. But the problem is still there.

Such a careful and quiet critic as Saville R. Davis of the *Christian Science Monitor* feared, after a recent year in Asia, that the most vulnerable spot in American foreign policy was its familiar alliance with the *status quo* in countries distinguished for graft and boodling and the personable profiteers with excellent appetites who always seem to be first in line when foreign aid arrives. We seem to feel that in these charming but feudal backwaters or countries run by tropical strongmen that aid must be channeled through the local panjandrum and his courtiers, the petty potentates and the handful of educated élite. Many of these have a shaky claim on the loyalties of their people. Often we are feeding the fat cats, and this can be a dangerous thing in a hungry world. "Corruption is rife," said Mr. Davis, "and the Americans are having the issue hung around their necks."

Both Messrs. Davis and Bowles argue for associating ourselves, where there is an alternative, with "the new representatives of the Asia of peaceful change," those who are trying to do something about land reform, black markets rigged for the privileged few, better health and education, and the things that really count.

Meanwhile, what to do? Perhaps the simplest solution for anyone, while working toward these goals, is to get on with the job at hand. The new countries of Africa and Asia are no place for perfectionists. Rather they need a lot of patience and a little time. I have always felt that even if some beggars are professionals and even if charity is only a partial and often inefficient answer, there is no point in refusing a hungry man while waiting for the millennium of fair shares and perfected distribution.

This dilemma was sharply illustrated by a teacher crisis in Laos: when with the help of foreign aid, teachers were trained for 150 village schools, some 350 other villages immediately built their own schoolhouses in the hopes that they could have teachers, too (so much for the article of faith that the Lao are predestined lotus eaters). But it takes six years to train a teacher. Comrade agents from the Pathet Lao began to turn up in the villages saying, "See, the Americans bring you soldiers and policemen. If you'll let us liberate you, we'll bring you *teachers*." One of the heads of the American economic mission in Vientiane was planning to send out bonzes from the Buddhist monasteries—young men with the relatively narrow classical theological training, but teachers all the same—until a new generation of teachers could be created.

It is here in the fields of education, agriculture, health, communications, and the rest, I feel, that the American and other sorts of foreign aid can make their most useful contribution. In some countries this sort of aid may be the only one entirely acceptable. Recalling Lenin's famous observation that the road from Moscow to Paris lies through Peking and Calcutta, a former legal adviser to the American embassies in India, Pakistan, Indonesia, Burma, Afghanistan, and Nepal named Matthew J. Kust wrote to the New York *Times:* "Communism is now firmly established in Peiping. It is waiting to reach Calcutta. Then Cairo, Baghdad and so on through Asia and Africa. Not by war but by political and economic means. . . . Meanwhile we are ready for war and almost totally unprepared for the economic and political struggle which Marx and Lenin have decreed."

The flow of geopolitical currents may seem far away and unreal to the man on the street in Saigon or Singapore, but the issues of race and nationalism are very near. The scars of all the many years of indentured labor and sometime slavery, the foreign masters in the colonies, the condescension too often built into words like "boy" and "native" or "backward" and "underdeveloped," or even "civilized" and "primitive," these scars still smart. They are the products of the attitude that Graham Greene once called "the white sneer," though it has been enthusiastically adopted by a number of boors who happen to be colored.

The wounds of the past have a painful legacy in resentment and sensitivity to hurt, the violent reaction or criticism, the chronic suspicion of the white, ex-colonial West. There is, in Africa and Asia, understandably, keen interest and a good deal of approval when the man of color comes into his own in almost any part of the world, and by almost any means, as the Japanese militarists showed with the degree of support they got for their "Greater East Asia Co-Prosperity Sphere" even after Manchuria, China, Pearl Harbor, and their occupation of a good part of Asia.

Intense racial prejudice is a relatively new thing in the world, in great part a child of colonial expansion in Asia, and the African slave trade that began in the fifteenth century, fed with the comfortable myths that stilled the consciences of the blackbirders and their customers. They reasoned that the slaves had been rescued from savagery and barbarism. Then there was the old argument that the colored peoples of Asia and Africa were incapable of governing themselves. There were the economic justifications of the opium trade, and all the rest.

If the distinction of color is an artificial one, still it exists, and is accepted as a concept by the colored peoples as well as by the white ones who invented it. Given an issue involving race, there can be a remarkable similarity of reaction among people of color from Peking to Djakarta to Johannesburg. News of racial violence in the United States goes round the world overnight, and it is difficult to explain that this reaction, this striking out by the lastditchers, who *are* on the losing side, is in a way reaction toward the progress Negroes are making. The accumulation of resentment over the years at the obvious bias against Asians in US immigration law —just to pick one sore point—makes suspicion of the United States difficult to overcome in any matter where color is concerned. (The immigration quotas for both China and India, with the two greatest populations in the world, were exactly zero for a long period before the Second World War, and are now a token 105 persons a year from each country.)

Curiously enough, Russia, politically, is somehow not considered by the Afro-Asian countries to be one of the white nations (wicked), though she certainly is mainly white, in spite of Mongol minorities. And the United States, while certainly the least "colonial" of the powers, is easily the favorite target of the anti-colonialists. These days, the usefully vague charge of "colonialism" means not just government of one country by another, but any sort of exploitation. In the Afro-Asian world, it is often restricted to white, Western exploitation. In spite of extraterritorial privileges in China and a number of Latin American interventions in the late nineteenth and early twentieth centuries (even Woodrow Wilson believed it was our moral duty to administer Haiti and the Dominican Republic, since these countries seemed incapable of governing themselves), the American temper has been fairly consistently opposed to colonial adventures, and the United States' own record as a colonial power has been brief, minimal, and relatively mild.

It is a long and complicated business, but I think that a great deal of this paradox can be traced to American racial attitudes, happily now changing. There is also a sort of guilt by association with the colonialists, all helped along by anti-American, anti-Western propaganda.

I believe this business of color is a central fact of life of our times. And I think it might be chastening and useful if we in the white part of the world would try not to forget the sensitiveness of that other part of the world—where most of the people live, and where, as Peggy Durdin has written, to be white "is generally a slight-to-very-considerable disadvantage."

"In Asia," said the Rev. Winburn T. Thomas at the 1953 assembly of the National Council of Churches Division of Foreign Missions, "colonialism is a bigger issue than Communism—and white is the color of colonialism." Dr. Thomas reported that Protestant church leaders in Java had declared themselves unanimously against the practice of sending out white missionaries almost exclusively, yet nearly ninety-nine per cent of American missionaries were white. Dr. Thomas' namesake, Madathilpara Mammen Thomas, an Indian student at Union Theological Seminary, at the same assembly warned against equating Christianity with Western civilization, and against Christian support of conservative or reactionary elements: "The Christian opposition to Communism should express itself as a Christian concern for the social revolution."

As for the white man in Asia, "His color is not a sign of special privilege, but rather a badge (historical) of guilt," says Mrs. Durdin, and then she quotes an Asian elder statesman: "People accuse us of being anti-American. The fact of the matter is that we are simply allergic to Westerners."

In spite of all this, as I thought about it, the future didn't look to me to be too gloomy. Time and fairness could soothe the smarting, cool the anger. Irritation doesn't last forever, and nothing changes more than people. I remembered how a few years earlier Britain's name had been anathema in Palestine, close to it in India. Now, British-Indian and British-

Israeli relations were increasingly cordial. When Prime Minister Macmillan visited Delhi somewhat later in a glow of mutual good cheer, the Republic of India happily broke out the Union Jack for the first time since 1947. Until recently, in some circles in India at least, Uncle Sam has been the villain of the piece; now, this too seems to be changing.

We are not necessarily in opposition—often much less so than we think. The twenty-eight Afro-Asian nations which met at Bandung to launch themselves as a power in the world called for an end to colonial domination, and to discrimination because of race or religion, for greater economic opportunities, and for peace. What gives me hope is that, as Ambassador Bowles pointed out, "these values are less Marxist than they are Western or American; no more or less than a reflection . . . of the continuing American revolution for which Jefferson, Lincoln, Wilson and Roosevelt spoke so eloquently."

18 EPILOGUE—GOING HOME

THE weeks in the hospital slipped effortlessly, quietly by, and then one day I was surprised to be told that five of them had passed, and that I might think about going home for convalescence.

I had been thinking mostly about Laos. It was changing so quickly, I felt sad to be leaving without seeing more of the south of the country, of the Pathet-held areas of the north to see how the Lao genius for passive resistance in depth was holding up under Communist indoctrination in Samneua and Phongsaly; without having spent more time in the pagodas talking with the bonzes; without having learned to do a really sinuous *lamvong*.

At the corner of the Vientiane market place as Zima Wong was driving me and my liver out to the airfield that last morning, I suddenly remembered there had been a man selling red balloons, the first balloons I had ever seen in Laos. The first telephone book had appeared, with nearly two hundred entries in Vientiane, a handful in Thakhek, Savannakhet, and Paksé, none in Luangprabang. Smoky de Paul was the proud proprietor of a jeep fire engine—the first fire fighting apparatus in the kingdom. With the Green Spot pasteurized orange drink that had invaded Laos from the US West Coast via Thailand, there were cheap Chinese Communist fountain pens and other gadgets from the north appearing in the market. A Junior Chamber of Commerce was in the air, and one of their first moves was to install a number of battered oil drums, painted white and marked JC on some of the Vientiane street corners as trash cans. Unheard of. The day that the first Lao traffic policeman appeared standing on a tub at an intersection near Vat Sisakhet, nobody could quite believe it. They wore holsters with no pistols in them. Small cars appeared with "Bus" and "Taxi" written on their windshields. The old-fashioned pedicab in which two Lao or one moderate-sized foreigner sat on a small wooden bench beside the driver was giving way to the shiny nickel-plated, sunburst-painted Thai model in which the driver pulled his passengers in a snappy buggy behind. The drivers were learning a few words of English.

There was new money in circulation, too, drab, indifferently printed little bills issued by the American Banknote Company, replacing the large, beautifully lithographed and delicately colored notes of the French treasury, bedizened with exotic beauties and romantic ruins. Whatever the design, it was worth about thirty-five to the dollar in Laos, anywhere from seventy to a hundred in Bangkok and Hong Kong, and there was in evidence a group of new rich who profited on the legal exchange rate with rigged import-export deals. New bars and dance halls sprang up, a hennaed Hungarian from

Hanoi came down to open a French provincial restaurant, and planeloads of taxi girls began to arrive from Hong Kong, Bangkok, and Saigon.

Behind the boom town was the bright-yellow earth-moving equipment lined up in rows in the American compounds. The road from Vientiane to Luangprabang was slowly being restored. Genuine asphalt now stretched twenty-nine kilometers to Thadeua so the King could drive down in his limousine, ferry over, and pick up the railway which now ran nearly to the bank of the river, and in a private car travel down through Bangkok and Malaya to Singapore, there to take a ship for France. Where there had been a dozen or so Americans in Laos when I arrived, now there were perhaps a hundred. There would be three hundred. There was a new American aluminum prefab compound called Silver City, a name which had overtones of the Gold Rush and the Forty-Niners. And for the newcomers there were many more creature comforts; the head of the economic mission led the way with a hot shower, very popular with the American female contingent for hair washing ("I'm going to Carters' to have a bath—want to come?").

Still, there were reminders of the civil war, not yet settled, and the precarious position of Laos which had led to the sudden heightening of interest in the country, the infusion of foreigners and money and change; the small trees growing on the street where I usually had had my lunch were protected by fences made of barbed wire, and as I left, freshly scrubbed old gas masks were hung out to dry on a line behind The Bungalow.

We didn't know it then, but the two years of near-famine in parts of Laos were ending, the beginning of the end of the rebellion was in sight, and CARE's mission there was drawing to a close. Sam Ziskind, CARE's chief of Mission in Haiti, was plucked from his tropical island home and sent to take over the Laos mission for the duration. A gentle, scholarly type, from a small town near Boston, who spoke fluent French, Spanish, Creole, and Hebrew, he turned up in Bangkok and headed off in the direction of Laos with his hastily assembled baggage, including a Royal Stuart tartan steamer cap. I was still weak as a blind kitten, homesick for New York, and anxious to see my family again at Christmas. But I hated to leave CARE in Laos, just now when the baby was beginning to toddle.

A few months later CARE decided its Lao mission had been accomplished, and began to wind up its affairs. I felt most unhappy at this, and Wells Klein and I argued ourselves blue in the face trying to prove to our superiors in New York that Laos was the most important place on earth, and CARE's small contribution there one of the most significant we could make anywhere. Patiently the facts of life were explained to us: in a changing world, CARE tried to remain flexible enough to help where best it could. The famine in Laos was now over, and there were countrywide feeding programs in Ceylon and Bolivia, Yugoslavia and Egypt, including the Gaza Strip. In the unforeseeable future lay a new self-help program in Poland, beginning with a couple of artificial-limb-making machines; and a two-million-dollar crash program of emergency relief for the Hungarian refugees across the frontiers in Austria and Yugoslavia and in Budapest itself. There was work in India and Hong Kong—and when I first saw the living dead of the Calcutta slums and the tubercular tenements and the fisher folk of Hong Kong, I agreed.

I still think Laos is important. Not dramatic, but quietly important, there on the dividing line between Indian and

Chinese cultures, beginning to stir drowsily and look at the outside world, East and West, mechanical, spiritual and creative, attractive and unfamiliar, comical and fearful. I hope the outside world will come to know the Lao, and that we may have the imagination and sense to learn something from them.

ACKNOWLEDGEMENTS

A THOUSAND and one special thanks are due my wife Bertie who dealt deftly with questions and crotchets, who ate, drank, dreamed and lived Laos in the years this was being written. To those at CARE and USIS and Air Laos, in the American and Lao governments and elsewhere, whose job it is to help but who went far beyond the call of duty, many, many thanks. A good many of them appear in the course of the story. Among those who helped especially were Max Finger, Elaine Heffernan, Hermie Michael, Betty Oliver, Pete & Pet Pettengill, Samar Sen, Henry & Swarn Selz, Drs Karl Schmidt & Kenneth Starr, Dr Mary Slusser and C. Sumner Stone, jr, all of whom gave me time and patience and better understanding.

Oden Meeker

NEW DELHI
NOVEMBER, 1958

BIBLIOGRAPHY

ABHAY, THAO NHOUY. *Aspects du Pays Lao.* Éditions Comité Littéraire Lao, Vientiane, 1956.

BATES, MARSTON. *Where Winter Never Comes.* Charles Scribner's Sons, New York, 1952.

BENOIT, PIERRE. *Le Roi Lépreux.* Albin Michel, Paris, 1927.

BERVAL, RENÉ DE (editor): *Presence du Cambodge.* France-Asie, numbers 114–115, Saigon, 1955.

———— *Présence du Royaume Lao.* France-Asie, numbers 118–119, Saigon, 1956.

BOWERS, FAUBION. *Theatre in the East: A Survey of Asian Dance and Drama.* Thomas Nelson & Sons, New York, 1956.

BOWLES, CHESTER. *Ambassador's Report.* Victor Gollancz, Ltd., London, 1954.

BRIGGS, LAWRENCE PALMER. *The Ancient Khmer Empire.* The American Philosophical Society, Philadelphia, 1951.

CARTER, T. D., with J. E. HILL and G. H. H. TATE. *Mammals of the Pacific World.* Macmillan, New York, 1946.

COEDÈS, G. *Les États Hindouisés d'Indochine et d'Indonésie.* E. de Boccard, Paris, 1948.

———— *Pour Mieux Comprendre Angkor.* Adrien Maisonneuve, Paris, 1947.

DANAUD, J.-P. (editor). *Cambodge* (album). Société Asiatique d'Éditions, Saigon, 1956.

———— *Indochine Profonde* (album). Revue Sud-Est Asiatique, Saigon, 1954.

DEYDIER, HENRI. *Introduction à la Connaissance du Laos.* Imprimerie Française d'Outre-Mer, Saigon, 1952.

EVANS, HAROLD (editor). *Men in the Tropics*. William Hodge and Company Limited, London, 1949.

FALL, BERNARD B. *The Viet-Minh Regime* (revised edition). Institute of Pacific Relations, New York, 1956.

GINSBURG, NORTON S. (editor). *Area Handbook on Laos*. University of Chicago, 1955.

GOVERNMENT OF INDIA. *Geneva Conference, Indo-China: Documents*. New Delhi, 1954.

HAMMER, ELLEN J. *The Struggle for Indochina*. Stanford University Press, Stanford, 1954.

LOVERIDGE, ARTHUR. *Reptiles of the Pacific World*. Macmillan, New York, 1956.

MALRAUX, ANDRÉ. *La Voie Royale*. Grasset, Paris, 1930.

MARCHAL, HENRI. *Angkor*. Albert Guillot, Paris, 1955.

MATHESON, MARION H. *Indo-China, a Geographical Appreciation*. Department of Mines and Technical Surveys, Ottawa, 1953.

MAY, REGINALD le. The Culture of South-East Asia. George Allen & Unwin Ltd., London, 1954.

MEZERIK, A. G. *Economic Aid for Underdeveloped Countries*. International Review Service, volume 3, number 35, New York, 1957.

PARMENTIER, HENRI. *l'Art du Laos*. 2 volumes. École Française d'Extrême-Orient, Hanoi, 1954.

PRICE, A. GRENFELL. *White Settlers in the Tropics*. American Geographical Society, New York, 1939.

ROMULO, CARLOS P. *The Meaning of Bandung*. University of North Carolina Press, Chapel Hill, 1956.

ROUX, HENRI. *Quelques Minorités Ethniques du Nord-Indochine*. France-Asie, numbers 92–93, Saigon, 1954.

SANDERSON, IVAN T. *Living Mammals of the World*. Hanover House, New York, 1956.

SASORITH, KATAY DON. *Le Laos*. Éditions Berger-Levrault, Paris, 1953.

SAVANI, A. M. *Visages et Images du Sud Viet-Nam*. Imprimerie Française d'Outre-Mer, Saigon, 1955.

SITWELL, OSBERT. *Escape With Me!* Macmillan, London, 1949.

THOMAS-DURIS, R., with KEOLA KHAMSOUK and SAYACOCIE KOU-KEO. Lexique Franco-Laotien à l'Usage des Élèves Infirmiers. Imprimerie du Gouvernement Royal, Vientiane, 1947.

THOMPSON, VIRGINIA, with RICHARD ADLOFF. *Minority Problems in Southeast Asia*. Stanford University Press, Stanford, 1955.

INDEX